Ruby Slippers
COOKBOOK

LIFE, CULTURE, FAMILY, AND FOOD AFTER KATRINA

Amy Cyrex Sins

Ruby Slippers

COOKBOOK
LIFE, CULTURE, FAMILY AND FOOD AFTER KATRINA

Published by Amy Cyrex Sins

For more information address cookbook@rubyslippersnola.com.

Ruby Slippers Cookbook, Life, Culture, Family and Food After Katrina contains a collection of recipes, which are not necessarily original to the author.

First Edition 2006

Book Design: Amy Cyrex Sins
Text Editor: Paulette J. Beatty
Photograph Editor and Cover Designer: Aaron L. Cyrex
Photography Consultant and Lead Photographer: Tate J. Tullier

Library of Congress Control Number: 2006904260

ISBN: 0-9785147-0-X

Dedication

To my wonderful husband, without whose support, I could not have made it through this mess or completed this project.

Acknowledgements

It is impossible to thank each person individually who has made a difference in our lives during this time. I will only mention a few.

I would like to take this opportunity to thank my dear family and wonderful friends, old and new, whose kind words, hard work and inspiration made each day a little easier. I'd also like to thank the people of Burnham Bible Baptist Church and Dr. Christos Ballas whose unselfishness and genuine care for others should be an inspiration to us all. To Mr. Steve and Stacy, we can never thank you enough for opening your home to us. And to Nik, thanks for the little things, they make me smile everyday. Beth, you helped me keep my sanity! And to AZ, thank you for caring about people and for making life easier during this tough time for your employees. And lastly, I offer my sincere thanks to my mom who was there for me every step of the way. Without you, this never would have been possible. I can't thank you enough!

IN MEMORY OF MY FATHER
DOUGLAS RICHARD CYREX
WHO LOVED HIS LITTLE GIRLS MORE THAN ANYTHING

TABLE OF CONTENTS

Foreword... ix

No Place Like Home... xi

Daddy's Jambalaya...xii

CHAPTER 1
Ruby Slippers
1

CHAPTER 2
New Year's Day
19

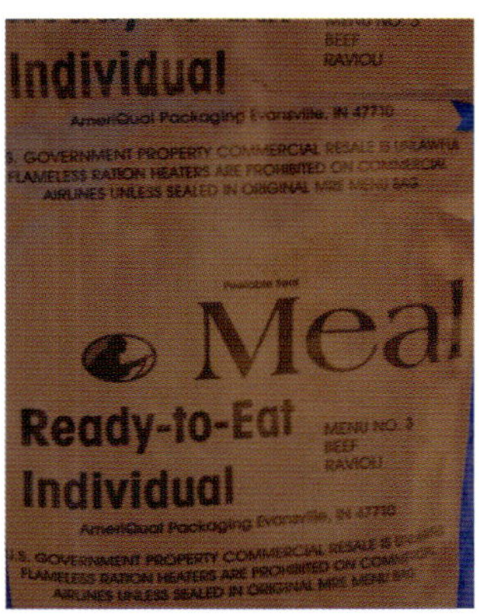

CHAPTER 3
Romantic Dinner for Two or Twenty
29

CHAPTER 4
Parade Route
41

CHAPTER 5
Repent It's Lent
51

CHAPTER 6
When the Saints Go Marching In
61

CHAPTER 7
Crawfish Boil and Sweet Dough Pies
71

CHAPTER 8
Cinco De Mayo
83

CHAPTER 9
Lakefront Picnic
93

CHAPTER 10
Ladies Tea Party
103

CHAPTER 11
Sweet Indulgence
115

CHAPTER 12
One Potato, Two Potato, SweetPotato
125

CHAPTER 13
The Outdoor Report
135

CHAPTER 14
Wash Day
145

CHAPTER 15
Family Dinner
155

CHAPTER 16
Sunday Brunch
165

CHAPTER 17
Holiday Gift Party
175

CHAPTER 18
Buffet Holiday Dinner
187

CHAPTER 19
Lagniappe
197

Eight Months Later- 209

Coalition To Restore Coastal Louisiana- 211

Resources- 214

Contributions- 215

Index- 216

THEODORE FONVILLE WINANS

Fonville began his career as a professional photographer in the late 1930's and for over fifty years traveled the highways and byways of South Louisiana photographing the people and places that define this unique and diverse culture. His many celebrated images have appeared in numerous publications including a book on his life and work entitled Fonville Winan's Politics, People, and Places.

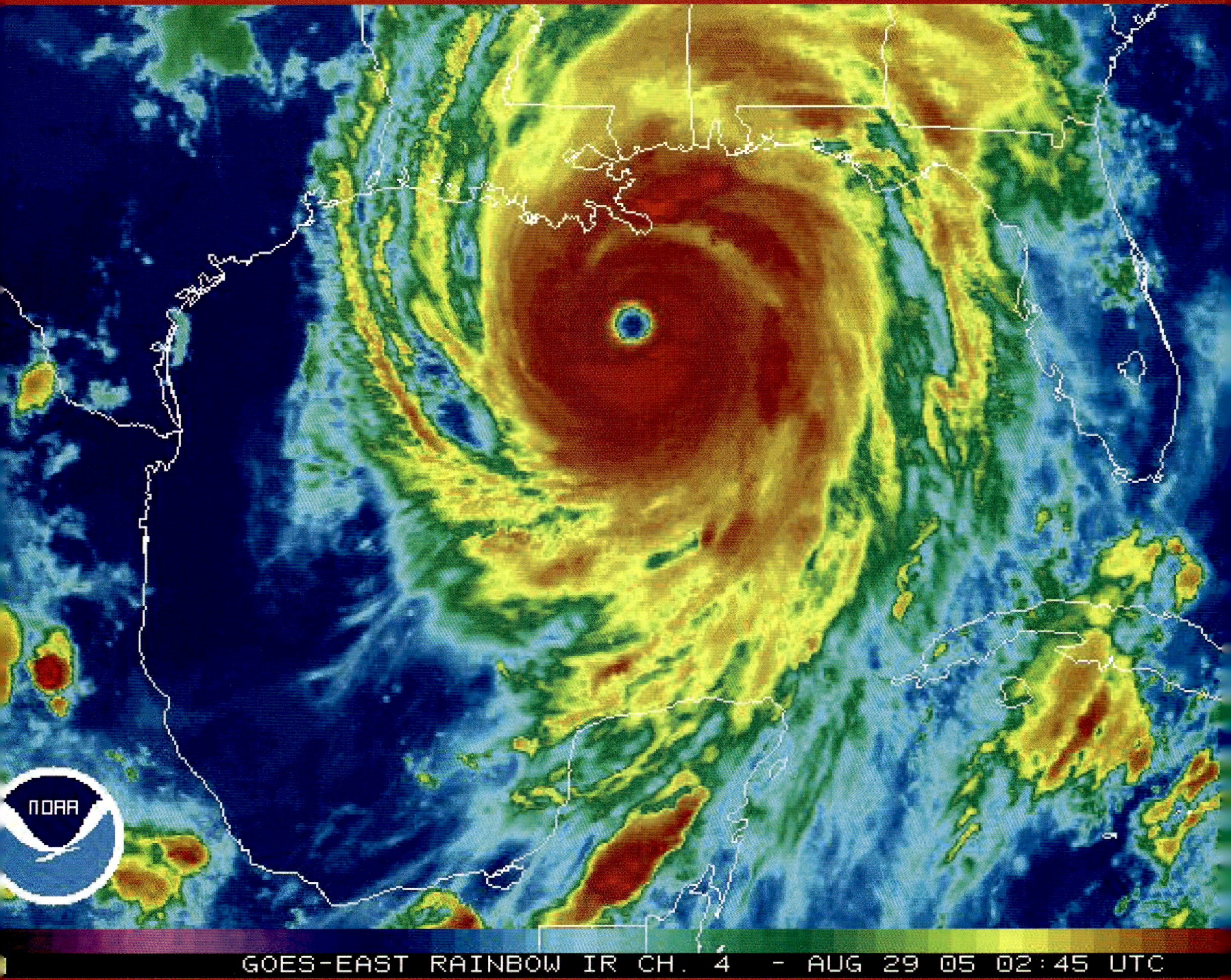
NOAA
GOES-EAST RAINBOW IR CH. 4 - AUG 29 05 02:45 UTC

Foreword by: Gaspar J. "Buddy" Stall

Because of the unprecedented destructive double whammy caused by both flooding and winds of Hurricanes Katrina and Rita, in time hundreds of books will be written about America's greatest tragedy. Eighty percent of the City of New Orleans was under water, not because of nature's wrath, but because of the Corps of Engineers' ineptness when building the levees and the Federal Government's procrastination in dealing with coastal erosion. Hundreds of thousands of New Orleanians were displaced to forty-two different states, and after seven months, the majority (estimated 80%) of those displaced are still residing outside their homes with no immediate relief in sight.

In all fairness, those who live and work outside the destruction area, even though you have watched it for hours and hours on television, unless you have seen it with your own eyes, you really have no idea of the magnitude of the damage.

Almost all of the books reference Katrina and Rita will no doubt pictorially and verbally describe the unequalled human sufferings of people from Texas to Alabama.

Amy Sins, in writing her book tells of not the Phoenix rising from the ashes but her personal story of making her way through her home that had eight feet of water plus two to three feet of the slimiest, smelliest, ungodly mud God has ever put on earth. You can imagine the shock in going into a site like that and see that everything you loved amassed in your lifetime is completely lost.

Amy shares her personal experience with dealing with the aftermath of Katrina and Rita, but her focal point is the City's fabulous food with the all-important need of passing down family recipes from generation to generation. It is her way of sharing with her readers and at the same time maintaining her sanity. As lagniappe, she includes a large and varied number of recipes for her readers to try. In doing so, they would be reminded of one of the unique things of New Orleans, its food.

Just as masters like Rembrandt, Michael Angelo and Leonardo Davinci, using paintbrushes and chisels could bring their paintings and statues to life, Amy has mastered words to the point one feels they are there. It is presented in an enjoyable, easy to read format. I am confident that after reading Ruby Slippers, you will be anxious as I to recommend it to your family and friends. For every misfortune there is always good fortune.

Amy's book falls into the latter category. New Orleanians love their food, be it an elegantly served seven course meal on china and crystal with linen napkins at Antoine's, the world's oldest family restaurant, located in New Orleans, or a simple seven course meal consisting of a cold six pack of Dixie Beer and a sloppy roast beef with an abundance of paper napkins.

New Orleanians love of food could be summed in the following. A man who worked in Atlanta, Georgia, called to tell his father he was coming in for a visit. He asked how long he planned on being in town. His response, sixteen meals.

In addition to having some of his favorite dishes only his mother can prepare, he requested reservations be made for him and his wife at Casamento's for an oyster loaf, Mothers for their fabulous breakfast, brunch at Begue's in the Royal Sonesta, stuffed seafood artichoke at Carmine's, fried chicken at Mr. Ed's, barbeque at Hillbilly Bar-B-Q, catfish at Adams Catfish House, soul food at Dooky Chase, prime rib at the Rib Room at the Royal Orleans, and emphatically requested that his last meal be a sloppy roast beef at Buddy's in Metairie, and if time allowed, he wanted to go to Donaldsonville to eat some Cajun food at The Grapevine.

As someone once reported, New Orleanians don't eat to live, they live to eat.

As Amy so ably points out, our home and professional recipes are city treasures and should be preserved for future generations. Yes, Rita and Katrina might knock us down but they will never knock out our taste buds.

Laissez les bon tons roulet and Bon Apetite!

Gaspar J. "Buddy" Stall

During our lifetime we are all asked to make a toast at a wedding, graduation or some other special occasion. The following is a sure fire winner:

May I wish each and every one of you every day of your lives steal, swear and lie.

Steal a little time every day to help those less fortunate; swear to do only those things right in the eyes of the Lord, and be sure to lie in the arms of the one you love every night and tell them you love them.

No place like home...

When many people think of New Orleans, they think of Bourbon Street and Mardi Gras. They think of good food and a few too many drinks. They think of dirty streets and maybe a little too much crime. But when I hear "NEW ORLEANS" I smile because New Orleans is my way of life.

When you live here, it's your heartbeat, and it's your soul. You feel the rhythm, and you breathe the spirit. You either love it or hate it; there is simply no in-between. When you live here, you are New Orleans! You are part of the spice in this great gumbo of a city.

Where else can you hear music everywhere you turn? Where else can you dress in costume in February and have people understand why? Where else is there a fabulous restaurant on every corner, but you know the best chef is your momma? Where else do you say, "Trow me sumpin mista," and you get something?

Only in New Orleans can you get a French fry po-boy smothered in debris gravy. Only in New Orleans can you "make groceries" or "let'em have it." Only in New Orleans can you buy tickets to a professional football game but show up wearing a bag on your head. And only in New Orleans will a toddler, teenager or grandparent know the dance when someone waives a napkin in the air.

Where else do the people maintain such hope after being struck down again and again? New Orleans has its own irreplaceable mix of the exciting and the unforgettable that makes the city so great. Who doesn't want to experience live jazz music or taste Remoulade? And who doesn't want complete strangers to welcome them like family?

I can't imagine being without the city that I love, but that's what almost happened in August 2005. I only hope that everyone else can't imagine it either. What a deficit there would be to live in a world without New Orleans!

As every day passes, I long for a return to the easier times when food and family were my way of life and worries were never an issue, a time when recipes were cherished and meals were shared with loved ones. Several events after Hurricane Katrina inspired me to work on this book, and several kept me going through the tough times.

While collecting recipes for this book, I met many fascinating and wonderful people along the way. Many had stories to share about New Orleans, Louisiana, family, and cooking. One story stands out as the most dear to my heart, and I'd like to share it with you.

Daddy's Jambalaya

Like most everyone in Lakeview, George and his family lost just about everything they owned when the levee broke. During their first trip back to their home, about a month after Katrina, George's wife Kathleen brought with them a list of things she wanted to find and hopefully salvage. George, on the other hand, brought no list and considered anything salvageable as a bonus.

The two of them were able to recover dishes, china, some crystal, and a few personal items and most of Kathleen's list. Surprisingly, a few of George's handwritten recipes survived, including his favorite recipe for jambalaya.

This particular recipe is special for several reasons, not the least of which was that it tastes great, but mostly because it was a recipe given to him by his brother-in-law, Doug, who passed away several years ago.

Doug gave him the recipe when George was first learning to cook. The recipe survived, but many of the handwritten notes and questions written on the page didn't. Those questions were, "How brown should the browned chicken be?" or "How much kitchen bouquet?" and "WHAT IS KITCHEN BOUQUET????"

As George held the recipe and pondered his discussions with Doug, he remembered that with Doug's instruction the first batch was great, and every batch after that was even better. It quickly became the family's favorite meal.

As important as the hand written recipe is to George, and as happy as he was to find it, he decided that it would mean a lot if he could pass it along to one of Doug's daughters. And he did.

George was right, that recipe means much more to me than he could ever know. Doug, my father, was a wonderful man with a terrific sense of humor, and I miss him greatly. He was a brilliant home chef who made cooking interesting, fun and memorable. I've spent the last six months trying to recreate his Jambalaya from taste and couldn't get it quite right, but now I can.

Thanks Uncle George!

Doug's (Daddy's) Jambalaya

1 chicken
2 cups long grain rice
1 onion, diced
3 3/4 cups water
2 cups rice
salt
pepper
garlic powder
Kitchen Bouquet

Cut chicken into pieces and brown in cooking oil. Remove chicken from pot and remove excess oil. Dice onion and add it to the pot to brown. Add 1/4 cup water and simmer onions in water until all of the water is gone. Add 1 cup of water, a touch of Kitchen Boquet and the chicken. Mix it up and bring it to a boil. Then add 3 1/2 cups of water and bring it back to a boil. (Always use 1 3/4 cups of water per cup of rice) Then mix two cups of rice into the pot and add salt. Always oversalt this dish! Add pepper and garlic powder. Mix and bring to a boil. Turn the stove down to a simmer.

The secret- DO NOT REMOVE THE LID for at least 20 minutes, 25 minutes is better!
C'est Bon!

Ruby Slippers

There's no place like home; there's no place like home. That's what I found myself thinking as I watched the events of Hurricane Katrina unfold. I just wanted to click my heels together and go back home, the way it was when I left: comfortable, predictable and certain.

I'll never forget the start of the series of events that would cause my life to change forever. The weekend of August 29, 2006, I was supposed to be on a relaxing and fun-filled weekend with my best friend from college, a weekend of pampering myself at a fancy spa in Chicago, a weekend of laughing and talking about days past and a weekend of dreaming about the future. Unfortunately, it wasn't as relaxing as I had planned.

On Saturday morning, my friend Beth and I were on our way to the spa for the best hot stone massage of our lives when my cell phone rang; it was my husband George calling from New Orleans to tell me that he was planning to evacuate early to avoid the traffic. A storm was approaching in the Gulf, and he was calling for packing instructions since I wasn't there to help.

Because we had been through this scenario once already this season, I told him "Bring the cats, my laptop and planner. Everything else should be fine for a few days until we get back in town. Make sure you check on my Paw Paw and bring him with you if Mom is already out of town. Love ya babe, I'm late for the spa. I'll see you on Sunday or Monday depending on my flight. Bye."

We continued our walk to the spa, and I started to think about how nonchalant we are about evacuating. We honestly can say we do it at a drop of a hat. Who wants to be without power, air conditioning, or cable TV? I've always thought the best choice is to get out of town and avoid the inconvenience. I'd rather an extra day of vacation in Chicago, and I know George would rather spend a little quality time with his grandmother. Besides, we already went through an uncomfortable experience with our first hurricane of the season. It was only a Category 1, and we didn't have electricity for almost four days.

Somehow, I couldn't help but get the nagging feeling, "Is this the one? Will it really hit New Orleans? Should I be worried?" I realized that there was nothing I could do about it; the situation was out of my control. I tried unsuccessfully to block what could happen out of my mind.

When we arrived at the spa, all I could talk about was the stupid hurricane. I shared with the manicurist the potential problems the city could face. She seemed genuinely surprised that such a scenario was possible.

I'm sure she was glad it was time for my massage after receiving a complete lecture on the need for coastal restoration, the up-the-mouth-of-the- river hurricane scenario and the effects of the oil and gas industry on the Louisiana coastline. She looked worn out by her environmental lesson and truly worried about the safety of New Orleans.

When I left, she wished me luck and said that I'd remain in her thoughts. "But really," I said, "what is the probability that would happen? One in a million? Relax, it won't be that bad."

When we returned to the hotel to freshen up, there was no weather channel or Internet access available to hotel guests. So, I had no idea how bad it really was. Finally, a member of the hotel staff was nice enough to pull up the Gulf Coast radar on their office Internet and print out a copy for me. It didn't look good. The pictures displayed a giant red mass in the middle of the Gulf of Mexico; panic finally set in!

I started calling friends and family telling them to get out of town. I called my co-workers to make sure they had a destination and a plan. I tried to urge my friend Steve to leave with his wife and two kids. Unfortunately, his plan was to wait and make a decision at the last minute. At that moment, his plan was to outrun the storm, which made me incredibly nervous! Then I started to think about me.

Where was I going to go? Here I am stuck in Chicago, and a category five hurricane is headed straight to my house. Not to mention, my flight home was scheduled to arrive in New Orleans at the exact moment the storm was going to hit.

When I called the airline, they said the only answer was to fly into New Orleans ASAP or wait it out in Chicago. The airline couldn't quite understand that if I arrived in New Orleans, there would be no one left in the city to pick me up at the airport! Were they not watching TV? Everyone was evacuating!

My options were few: stay at the Intercontinental indefinitely, stay with a friend of a friend of a friend that I did not know in Chicago indefinitely, fly to Louisville and stay with Beth indefinitely, or hope that I could get in touch with my sister in Houston and fly there.

The most reasonable idea was to fly to Houston and stay with my sister Susan and her family rather than paying for a high-priced hotel room or staying with a stranger. After dealing with several airline reservationists, I was able to book a flight from Chicago to Houston on Sunday afternoon. There was nothing to do but wait, and again I tried to get Katrina out of my mind. I needed support, and I turned to my friend Beth and turned to food.

Moto

Beth and I embarked on a dinner that would truly be my last in the world as I knew it. We planned the dinner for months, and there was no point in sitting around in the hotel watching CNN and worrying more. Everything was going to be fine; I was sure. Diversions are always good anyway. A trip to the imaginative restaurant Moto would surely raise my spirits.

The meal at Moto was the most interesting and exciting I've ever had. You might even say the chefs had dreams of being scientists. Or perhaps they were closet modern art majors who now use a tablecloth as a palette. Either way, it was incredibly interesting.

Appetizers that should be served hot, were served frozen, the chips and salsa resembled no chips and salsa I'd ever eaten, and the soup made you look like you were a smoke breathing dragon with every bite. The smells and the sights awoke the senses and challenged any preconceived ideas of how food should be served. It was so amazing; I photographed every plate of our meal! I couldn't wait to tell everyone about it.

The meal was certainly more adventurous than Beth expected. During the meal, we visited with the tables around us, relaxed and had fun. Of course, Katrina was still the topic of conversation, but the mood stayed light, and the other dinner guests were supportive. Everyone wanted to talk about New Orleans: the food, the music, the people and the bars. Everyone there "loved" New Orleans and had some wonderful story about visiting.

When things were rough during the following months, I found comfort in my fascinating culinary experience prior to Katrina and shared it with others.

Tostitos with Salsa Jelly and Margarita

Margarita Sorbet

2/3 cup sugar
1 teaspoon apple pectin
2/3 cup water
1 tablespoon glucose syrup
2 cups lime juice
1/2 cup orange juice
1/2 cup tequila

Mix sugar and pectin together and set aside. Pour water into a pot and add glucose. Heat over medium heat.

Tostitos

10-15 corn tortilla chips (large)
3 cumin seeds
2 black pepper seeds
1/2 lime, zested
1 cup vegetable of chicken stock
1 tablespoon cocoa butter
1 tablespoon glucose syrup
1 tablespoon salt
1 tablespoon lime juice

Moto Restaurant
945 W. Fulton market
Chicago, IL 60607
312-491-0058
www.motorestaurant.com

Toast chips with the spices in a pot over high heat. Add the stock and zest lime into the pot. Cook for two minutes. Pour mixture into blender and add cocoa butter, glucose, salt and lime juice. Puree for about two minutes until smooth. Ideally, this should be strained and chilled for an hour and slowly add the sugar-pectin mixture while whisking vigorously. When all the sugar has been added and the water reaches a boil, cook for two minutes on high heat. Cool mixture down until cool to the touch. Add citrus juices and tequila. Freeze in ice cream machine according to manufacturer directions.

Tomato Salsa Jelly

8 Roma tomatoes
1 Jalapeno
1/2-3/4 red onion
1 clove garlic
lime juice to taste
salt to taste
gelatin, 6 two gram sheets per 2 cups strained liquid

Soak gelatin in cold water. Cut tomato into quarters. Cut jalapeno in half and remove seeds. Cut onion into 1/4. Juice all vegetables through an electric juicer Add a generous pinch of salt and stir. Let the mixture sit for two hours or overnight. Strain through a coffee filter in a fine strainer. Let sit until fully drained (overnight is best.) Strained liquid should be clear. Season the liquid with lime juice and salt if needed. Strain once more through another coffee filter. Measure the amount of liquid to the nearest cup and reserve excess juice for other uses. Warm 1/4 cup of juice until hot to the touch. Add gelatin to warm liquid. Stir to dissolve. Add the remainder of juice and allow to chill for 3 hours. Cut into shapes and serve with chips and margaritas.

Katrina

I arrived in Houston on Sunday afternoon to my niece Kate's and nephew James' extreme excitement that their Aunt Amy showed up for a surprise visit. How could they be so lucky to have so many people arriving in Houston at the same time just to visit them? I can only imagine how popular those two young children felt having so many extra people in their home.

There were quite a few people in my sister's home. All arrived on a moment's notice because of Katrina: my sister, Susan, her husband Ray and their two kids, not to mention, her brother-in-law Bubba and his son Christian. Bubba's family was forced to separate from his family during the evacuation, and his wife and daughter were in another town. The musical sounds of children playing could be heard at all times. The children laughed at the way the "Y'at" talked and attempted to mimic the accent. It was comforting to have so much happiness around. That evening, we enjoyed a wonderful dinner of stuffed shrimp as a family. Susan and Ray went to great lengths to give us a little taste of home while we were there. The food and the company helped to calm our nerves.

I promised Kate, after dinner, that I would play dress up at some point during my visit if she went to bed on time every night. The conversation remained light, and everyone was trying to remain calm, but it was next to impossible.

Once the kids went to bed, the adults started the conversation that had been held back all day long. We talked at length about the impending storm. We knew that we were smarter than the weathermen. That storm wasn't really going to hit the mouth of the river. But what if it did? "Well then we would all have much bigger problems, so there was no point in worrying about it," we joked. But we all were worried.

Every couple of hours that evening, my husband urged me by phone to relax. He was safe with his parents and grandmother, but it was still difficult to relax with the storm heading straight to the city. The next few hours seemed like an eternity.

Bubba and I were awake most of the night just watching the radar and waiting to see where the storm would go next. After a couple of hours of restless sleep, I was once again glued to the television. I awoke to news reports, "New Orleans Spared" which was a stark contrast to what I had seen the day before, "New Orleans Doomsday." The reporters were walking through the Quarter, laughing and saying that New Orleans was in the clear and ready to return to normal. Boy, were they wrong!

I breathed a sigh of relief and relaxed for just a little while. I thought, "YEAH! We dodged a bullet again!" Katrina didn't hit the mouth of the river; instead it hit just to the east of us. That was a much better possible situation for the city, so we thought.

After lunch, we logged on to the Internet and started watching the live local New Orleans news. Unlike my husband, who was stuck in St. Francisville, LA with no electricity and Katrina bearing down, I had the luxury of air-conditioning, Internet, and television. Life was good, for a little while anyway.

When I went to bed that night, Kate was sleeping in my suitcase, in her little pink tulle dress right next to the bed. She was still waiting to play dress up, but went to bed on time like she promised. She looked so comfortable, carefree and happy; I wished I could go back in time when there were no worries in the world.

That night I actually slept. I believe the exhaustion and sleep deprivation had finally peaked, and my body shut down. I slept hard, really hard, but it could not prepare me for the days ahead.

The next morning I had major stress and issues to deal with, the only way cope was to cook and eat. I know you shouldn't turn to food in a situation like this. When all is said and done, maybe I can get counseling. But honestly, don't you always feel better after a home cooked meal, or that little something sweet? I know I do.

Online is where I heard the real story. The two local newscasters appeared as if they had been crying. I looked at my fellow evacuees, and said, "It seems as if they know something we don't know and it doesn't look good." And then one of the newscasters said, "Our homes are gone, and most of the city is under water."

Shortly after that online broadcast, I watched in horror at the national news. The sights of my hometown in chaos and very wet made the situation even more surreal. My thoughts were racing, "The levees broke? But how could that be? The storm didn't hit the mouth of the river! The levees should have held! Oh no, the levees should have held! This can't be happening! This is all wrong! We were spared! We were spared! It said so on the news! Oh dear God, what will we do now?"

At that moment, life became very dreamlike. But it wasn't a good dream; it was a nightmare. I saw my house! I saw the water! I was glued to the television, and it felt like time stood still. My husband was somewhere with no electricity, no television and no way to communicate. I knew what was going on, and he didn't, and it was making me crazy. I needed him with me, right then, to help me face this situation!

My house was on the national news all day. It was exactly ten houses from the levee break on the 17th Street Canal. The news footage helicopter continuously flew over the break and then my house. I could see the water; I could see the roofline. But I couldn't tell how deep the water was, only that my house was flooded.

And so I started cooking. Bubba's son Christian was enlisted in kitchen patrol to help satisfy my cravings. The first order of business, bake a cake! And so we did. We baked the best cake in the world. It was a Chocolate, Chocolate, Chocolate Cake. And then we ate until life became good again!

There is something about a messy chocolate smile on a young boy's face, after you tell him he can lick the bowl, which makes you feel that everything is going to be OK.

After enjoying the cake, I began what had become my daily routine. I pulled up a chair and watched TV and waited to see something that would give me hope. As I sat transfixed on that little box of moving pictures, Kate walked up to me with her magic wand and dressed in the pink tulle dress. She knew that I was upset and that the TV had something to do with it. She looked at me and then walked to the TV and said, "Poof, no more bad water! Time to play and have fun."

How could I resist that? I finally agreed to play dress up. Little Kate thought she hit the jackpot when she saw all of my dress up clothes. After all, I had packed like a diva. It was a girl's weekend complete with a black sequined top and snakeskin heels. It was perfect for Kate's idea of dress up, whereas at the time, I would have killed for a pair of sweats and some tennis shoes. We played princess, we played rock star, we played just about every famous exciting thing a four year old could dream up, and in the middle of it, my husband called.

Finally, George got through! We could talk!

The storm had knocked out all cellular towers, flooded local phone lines and completely halted all forms of communication. So many people were attempting to dial at the same time, all of the available active lines where overwhelmed. If your family didn't have the benefit of a teenager, it was almost impossible to communicate. It was apparent early on that the only form of communication was text messaging which, my husband and his family had never attempted, and without which there was no communication. Thank God for teenagers who were proficient in text messaging. We could never thank them enough.

While turning the sequined top in to a kid's size dress, I answered the phone, and for the first time was forced to face reality with my husband. It was awful. I felt guilty because, I was finally paying attention to Kate and not the television, and the phone had to ring. It was obvious that she was tired of all this grown up stuff that was no fun! But I needed my husband so I could talk and cry and have some comfort.

That night, I decided to sit down, have a glass of wine, a piece of chocolate cake and assess my situation. It is amazing what you think of when facing tragedy and disaster. The first order of business, check on the people, second, what about the pets? Third, the future.

My first thoughts were, "What is going to happen? Did everyone get out of town? What about Steve and his family? I thought of just about every person I have ever been in contact with during my time in New Orleans. I worried about their welfare. Is my home really gone? Is everything I know and love gone?" I prayed for everyone's safety. I prayed like I have never prayed before.

I knew my husband had evacuated and was safe, and most of my family had checked in by text message. I felt fortunate that I was safe. I had some clothes, money, and most of all I had a family that loved me. At that moment, I realized I could get through this; we could all get through this.

Perhaps it was the lack of sleep, maybe it was the stress of the situation, or maybe it is just what happens during times like these, but I was living in a daze. I no longer had any concept of time, and I had nothing but time. The hours and days were running together. I had been sitting at the kitchen table with a blank note pad for hours trying to plan my future.

It was the first time during this ordeal that I realized that all I had were questions, and that the answer to each one was the same, uncertain. I thought about what I would miss, if I could never go home: my friends, my way of life, everything I own, and the city I love. Yet again, my thoughts were racing. I started thinking, about my childhood and recent past and the things I remember and know and love about New Orleans that could be gone forever.

The Plan

The next step was to get to my husband. I couldn't fly there, I didn't have a car, and he couldn't really come and get me.

Houston was nice; I appreciated the hospitality and reassurance of everyone I met, and I did enjoy spending time with Susan and her family, but I wanted my husband.

Thankfully, a nice neighbor of Susan's showed up at her house one morning a little more than a week after the storm. He said, "Amy, you let me know when you are ready, and I'll drive you to Lafayette, and your husband can meet us there."

I didn't mean to appear so eager, but I told him I could be ready in 10 minutes. I will forever hold a special place in my heart for John. Thank you for driving four hours with a crazy woman to see her husband. And thank you for not sticking around to watch her breakdown in the parking lot when she finally could hug him.

It would be easy to feel sorry for myself if I were the only person in the world dealing with this tragedy, but that was not the case. Hundreds of thousands of people have been touched by this event, and I am lucky that everyone that I know and love survived.

Prairieville

There was a time in my life that I didn't appreciate what I had, a quiet easy life, surrounded by family in a small town. Instead, I wanted to get away from it and go to the big city, New Orleans. I wanted the hustle and bustle. I wanted nightlife. I wanted fancy restaurants and live music. I wanted to get out of small town America and make it on my own. And I did, only to return years later at the hands of Katrina and levee failures. And it was in returning that I realized what I took for granted for so many years. Everything. The one thing I needed was the quiet easy life one could only find outside of the city. The other thing I needed was to be surrounded by family that cared.

I experienced the kind of kindness and giving that happens in small towns across America, the kindness and giving that I know others in my situation experienced.

My husband and I realized that we were not going home anytime soon and that we needed to set up a temporary life for the cats and ourselves until we had a plan. We had no idea if anything in our home was spared and planned for the worst.

Our living options were limited: Move in with my mom in Baton Rouge and sleep on the sofa and recliner for potentially months or move in with my in-laws and join their post Katrina relocated life in St. Francisville. Both were solid options, but both would prove to be very crowded living arrangements.

We opted for plan C. Because of the kindness of my sisters, Randee, Laura and Aaron, living in Prairieville, we got started. They were able to set us up in a wonderful apartment above the garage of Randee's father-in-law's home.

When we saw it for the first time, it was overwhelming, completely stocked down to the silverware and bathroom towels. We had furniture, we had dishes, and we had pots and pans, we even Blue Plate Mayonnaise and Zatarain's Seasoning Mix. And we had wonderful neighbors! Every day we thanked God for our family!

Best of all, I could start cooking again! I think that our neighbors put on about ten pounds, as did we, with all of the leftovers I delivered to their door. Being with my husband made me happy. Cooking also made me happy, and I was delighted to have the chance to share my cooking with others.

What To Expect

I have learned that you can never be prepared enough for the shock of seeing your home and neighborhood for the first time after a devastating event. I assume that I felt similarly to those who face forest fires, tornadoes, earthquakes and man made disasters: overwhelmed.

We were certainly not realistic about what we could do when we entered our home for the first time. We could not drive a truck to our house because of the debris, so we had to take a four wheel ATV with a small trailer on the back. The debris was 20 feet high in some areas. A house, from three blocks away, had floated and landed in our driveway. There was a house in our driveway!

I couldn't see down my street because the trees were all fallen and piled together. Mounds of dirt, from the break in the levee, were piled up in the street. There were cars in trees, hot tubs in the middle of the park and roofing tiles everywhere.

The area was completely deserted, and everything was gray. There were no birds, there was no grass and there were no people. I didn't even see any mosquitoes! All signs of life appeared nonexistent, except for the occasional National Guard troops patrolling the area.

We drove past X's everywhere, busted roofs where people escaped and flooded out cars as far as the eye could see. I could tell my grandfather's neighbors were saved and so were the people down the street. I worried about the old man in the walker that lived four blocks away. I prayed that someone evacuated him and his little white dog.

The entire experience was like being in a black and white movie. It looked as if a bomb had gone off, but without the fire. I just looked around trying to find any shade of color other than gray.

When we finally navigated through the debris and saw our home, we were a little relieved to see that it was still there. The outside was very deceiving. The damage appeared to be pretty mild, but it wasn't.

I'm not sure what we were thinking, but we assumed that we would walk right up to the house, open the front door and grab a few things. Not a chance. When we reached the entryway, I looked through the dirty window. I could see the large ottoman for the sofa wedged against the door. It wasn't supposed to be there. I could also see the outdoor lawn chairs in our foyer; they weren't supposed to be there either.

We soon realized that opening the front door would prove an impossible feat and that climbing the piles debris on the side of the house and getting to the backyard would be the only option. We moved aside flowerpots, wood, bricks and things that were unidentifiable and then made our way into the backyard. Once there, we saw a barren landscape. Gone were the new plants, gravel paths and fence that were part of our newly designed backyard. All that was left was mud, dead plants and debris from someone's home. We found a Brittany Spears CD, stuffed animals and an ice chest that were not ours. We also noticed that our lawn furniture, flowerpots and garden accessories were not there! The large pecan tree was dead and lying on our shed. The fence was down and spread in every direction, and our back doors were gone.

Nothing looked like it did when George evacuated.

And then it hit us, the smell. It was awful! Some of you won't understand, but I can only compare it to a port-a-potty on the last day of Jazz Fest or Mardi Gras or worse. Yes, it was that bad, and we had to endure it to enter our home. The smell is so distinct that I can close my eyes far away from New Orleans and still smell it. I will forever smell mold when I think of my house.

With masks, rubber boots and gloves we climbed the debris on the back porch. There was a six-inch layer of black slimy mud throughout our entire home, and our doors were somewhere underneath it. Walking was treacherous because the mud was incredibly slippery.

Looking around I noticed that nothing was where I left it, and many of my belongings were unrecognizable. I had a table on my counter top, a sofa in my dining room, lawn furniture in my foyer and wet, muddy cookbooks everywhere. The cabinets were falling out of the walls, the curtains were somewhere under the mud, and glasses had floated all over the house.

Imagine filling your house up with water and pulling a plug so that everything whirlpools around until it lands. That is probably what happened in our home. A Sprite bottle had floated from the kitchen into the living room and was the only thing holding up a bookshelf full of encyclopedias. A canister from the kitchen full of sugar had somehow moved itself onto the top shelf of my entertainment center. It looked as if I had placed it there for decoration.

My house was turned upside down, and nothing was in its original place except the china cabinet. Maybe George was right when he said I had too many dishes. That can be the only explanation for only one piece of furniture staying exactly where we left it. Every glass was filled to the brim with a stinky, grayish-black, muddy Lake Pontchartrain cocktail.

The air was stagnant and took your breath away, even with a mask. And the mold was growing out of control like a fuzzy marine animal climbing our walls. I swear I could see it growing while we were looking around! The beautiful home I loved and poured my heart into was now nothing but a giant petri dish!

Our first order of business was to verify that the water didn't get into the second floor. Thankfully, it did not, and then we had to get creative. Another storm was on her way, and it was possible our home could take on more water in the future. We needed to get what we could and get out in about an hour or two. We needed to prioritize.

We realized early on that hauling our belongings through all of that debris was not an option. Clothes and linens were a priority because they were the lightest things to carry. Our solution was to drop them out of the second floor window. By lowering them out the window, we could avoid slipping in the mud and ruining the items we could save. My husband stood in the driveway as I filled garbage bag after garbage bag with clothes, towels and sheets and dropped them out of the window.

While throwing things into the driveway I began to think about George, my 6'5" and 260 pound husband, and his most recent Monday Night football experience. I laugh every time I think of my husband sitting about a foot from a 10-inch TV on a tray table in the living room of our Prairieville apartment trying not to miss a single play.

In all that heat, I came up with a brilliant idea! Save a TV, a VCR and a radio. Somehow I could engineer a system to lower them out of the window. I looked around the upstairs and was able to find a large duffle bag and a 100 foot extension cord.

I put a piece of electronic equipment into the duffle bag, tied it with the extension cord and lowered it very slowly into George's arms. I know we looked like looters! If only the National Guard had driven by then, they probably would have laughed at our clever engineering! But, victory would be sweet now that we were upgraded to a 19 inch television!

We loaded everything onto the four-wheeler and prepared to leave. We were happy that something was accomplished and that we had a better understanding of our challenges ahead. And now George could watch the Saints game on Sunday without a magnifying glass to read the score!

Rita

I could not have been the only person who felt like a hurricane magnet. It seemed that I could not get away, and they were following me. Only a few weeks after Katrina, Rita was on her way and just as big or bigger.

Here we go again! It may be going to New Orleans or it may be going to Houston, or somewhere in between. Yet more uncertainty!

Since we were in Prairieville, we didn't have to evacuate, but my sister in Houston did. Her husband was out of town on business, and she had to evacuate with the kids on her own. Just before she left, she asked me for advice, "What should I take with me?"

I said, "If money can't replace it, take it with you." And I meant that!

I suggested that she bring family pictures, artwork that her kids created, mementos from her childhood and any other keepsakes and heirlooms that she would miss dearly if gone. I also suggested that she take pictures of her house as she was leaving and grab any paperwork from her insurance company that she could possibly need. And then I told her to be careful and get on the road!

It took her 12 hours to drive from Houston to Prairieville. This is normally a five hour drive. And she made better time than most people!

In the meantime, we stocked up with supplies, water, can goods, batteries, and cereal. Somehow I convinced myself that I could live on Fruit Loops for a week or two if we were out of power. But, now that I think a little more clearly, I realize that probably was not the answer to potential hunger.

That night we had a nice steak dinner at home, a bottle of wine and hunkered down for the bad weather that was on its way. This time I was forced to listen to the wind whirl through the trees and the rain beat down on the roof.

The entire time I actually hoped that the hurricane would hit my house in New Orleans. I figured that our stuff was already ruined, so there would be less damage than if the storm hit an area that had been spared in Katrina.

As the wind roared and the rain poured, I tried to sleep, but it was almost impossible. I sat on pins and needles thinking that we'd have to worry about trees falling on the building. Luckily, we ended up making it through the night virtually unscathed.

When we went out the next day, we witnessed a lot of flooding in low lying areas, trees down and power outages. Yet another mess the people of Louisiana would have to clean up.

We watched the news as our hometown flooded again. But honestly, who cares? Everything was already wet anyway!

Western Louisiana took a big hit from this storm. Many people we know had sought refuge in Lafayette, LA and Beaumont, TX from Katrina, and my thoughts and prayers were now with them.

I began to wonder if Rita had caused the same type of destruction to the Cajun culture that Katrina had to New Orleans. Homes, people, histories, fisheries, oyster beds and crawfish farms could all be gone forever.

What an empty world this would be! No New Orleans? No Crawfish? No Oysters? No South Louisiana? I can only wish for it all to come back stronger than ever.

The Kindness of Others

Hurricane Katrina has been an emotional ordeal for us. The kindness of others made this situation much easier to face. Strangers provided us with clothing, supplies, and financial support and their thoughts and prayers. Each of these helped make our lives just a little bit easier.

There is one particular group of strangers that helped us more than we could imagine. A church group from Burnham, PA showed up at our house one day to help us cut down fallen trees. We never expected the group of six people with power tools, wheelbarrow and a strong will could get things done so quickly.

The caring people of Burnham Bible Baptist Church drove over 20 hours and took time out of their personal lives to help people throughout the New Orleans area. During their time in the Big Easy, they lived in a gymnasium with a hundred other volunteers and worked exhaustively to help the citizens get their homes cleaned up.

Not only did they help cut down fallen trees, but they also helped us strip our home of muddy debris, moldy sheetrock and soggy insulation. Anyone else may have turned and run when they saw the mess that was our garage. Instead, this wonderful group of people put on their masks, gloves and rubber boots to help us shovel a foot of mud out of our garage.

They didn't stop until the entire garage was done. Then after a brief po-boy buffet and jambalaya, they decided to tackle the cabinets and appliances. We never would have gotten so much work done without their help. Once we saw the entire home free of mold, mud and trash, we were given hope again that our lives could be rebuilt. We just needed to know if the city would allow us to start the process.

In Limbo

From that moment on, our lives became an eternal limbo. Yet again, the story and situation changed daily; but as always, the outcome remained the same: uncertainty! Can we rebuild? Will insurance cover the damages? What will happen with the levees? Will the government take our home to fortify the levee? Will we be able to get flood insurance again? When will we have answers?

Every day was a new challenge. We could only live in the moment, a life of confusion, stress and doubt. Planning was next to impossible. At any given time, we had at least two plans and a backup plan for those. Maybe we would stay in Prairieville; maybe we would move back; maybe we would buy a new house and sell the old one. But, who would want a flooded house? When all was said and done, I wanted to move back home to New Orleans.

I couldn't consider the possibility of not helping to rebuild a wonderful community full of life, culture and history. I would not consider missing out on the cuisine forever.

Once we made up our minds, we decided that no matter what, WE WILL RETURN HOME!

For months we could not get a straight answer from local officials. We called daily to the City and Army Corps to find out if rebuilding was possible. We asked if the local governments would turn our home into a new levee system. No one had an answer or an estimated time for us to receive an answer.

Meanwhile, we pay a mortgage for an unlivable home, and we wait! All we want are answers and the ability to move forward.

Finally, almost five months after the flooding, we called the Army Corps again, and this time, there was an answer. And, it was the one we wanted. "Go ahead, rebuild"

So the process started! Rebuilding and eventually moving home to start over in New Orleans would be a part of the "new normal."

The New Normal

Life in New Orleans is very different during this rebuilding phase. Every conversation starts with, "Before Katrina," and no one has anything else to talk about. Everywhere I look is a sign that says, "now hiring." The traffic is uncontrollable, and rent is outrageous. Very few stores are open late and very few restaurants have a full menu. Most people feel lucky to have hot water and gas service and even luckier if the blue tarp is still attached to their roof.

As I drive down the formerly flooded streets, I look at piles of debris rather than the homes. It is heartbreaking to see what was once someone's life all piled up on the curb. Baby beds, bikes, stuffed animals and toys line the streets covered in mold and mud. Entire dining room sets are placed on the "Neutral Ground" ready for Sunday dinner. The muddy plates, silverware and even a flooded bottle of wine are all arranged perfectly, as if to say, this was once a beautiful place where our family dined. It is incredibly hard to look past the trash; all I see is what was once someone's very pleasant life.

As a "Foodie" things were really different for me. Life in refuge outside of New Orleans made me appreciate what I had. I began to miss the wonderful neighborhood restaurants with high quality food. I missed the places where so many people gathered to visit and discuss happy times. Most of all, I missed good service, and I missed my waiters!

I missed going to a local restaurant and receiving the handshake or hug from the maitre'd when so often the tourists wondered if we were celebrities. I missed getting that smile from the staff that says, thanks to the locals for supporting and loving their business.

One thing I am learning to understand is that we can't go back to the way things were; we can only go forward and create a future. We must pick up the pieces, put them back together as best we can and move on into the "new normal."

If we follow the road back after Katrina, New Orleans will be a vibrant and colorful city once again. Hopefully soon, the levees will be improved, homes will be repaired, and we will move from this world of gray to Technicolor once more. Then we can all stop clicking our heels because we will be home.

There's no place like home in New Orleans!

New Year's Day

Black Eyed Peas

Panned Pork Chops

Smothered Cabbage

Creole Maque Choux

Cornbread

Nanny's Banana Pudding

Brandy Milk Punch

Bayonna:

Grilled Shrimp with Coriander Sauce

and Black Bean Cake

Stephen, Dawn and Baby Madelyn

Hurricane Katrina was fast approaching when Stephen and Dawn began discussing their plans.

During her last doctor's visit, Dawn was given a copy of her medical records by her physician, just in case she might need them. Her doctor also instructed that if things looked grim, Dawn should go to Memorial Hospital where generators and supplies would be available. Dawn's medical condition was somewhat fragile. Her baby was due at any minute, the baby was expected to be big, she had gestational diabetes, and complications were expected.

Stephen and Dawn suggested to their families to evacuate to Houston. They promised that if the weather escalated and they were without power, the couple would go to the hospital immediately.

On Sunday morning they awoke to a big change; Katrina had grown tremendously and was turning for New Orleans. They were beginning to get scared. Dawn's fragile nerves were even more frayed when no one answered the phone at her physician's office.

The hospital suggested that Dawn and Stephen leave town. They evaluated the traffic situation and assumed it was better to go west towards Florida.

They packed the car with the hospital overnight bag, a car seat, three days of clothes, a little traveling food, and Barkley, their golden retriever and headed towards Florida.

Dawn furiously called hotels as Stephen drove them to safety. They were fortunate to find two hotels with openings, one in Pensacola and one a little closer to New Orleans. They were a little worried about traveling too far in with Dawn's condition but decided that the extra thirty minutes away from New Orleans would be a better decision, so they chose the hotel in Pensacola.

Dawn believed that she was having contractions during the drive, but was determined to make it out of harm's way. Once they reached the hotel, they were exhausted and ready to sleep. Their hotel lost electricity and only had peanut butter and jelly to eat. They waited out the storm and received a call from a friend about the turmoil in New Orleans. The friend suggested that they get to a hospital immediately because returning home soon would not be an option.

Searching for an available hospital proved to be more difficult than searching for an available hotel. The two traveled to Birmingham where a family member had arranged for medical care and a physician to deliver Dawn's baby. They arrived on Thursday and consulted with a doctor on Friday. Luckily, she had all the medical records that she needed.

By Monday, Dawn was in labor and by Tuesday, beautiful baby Madelyn was born.

Though their experience was scary and unfortunate, the couple easily looks past it. Every time Dawn gazes upon Madelyn's beautiful face, she is overwhelmed with happiness and has proof that something perfect can result from a terrible situation.

Black Eyed Peas

"I always serve anything like this with Crystal Hot Sauce and cornbread."
Karen

1 pound dry black eye peas (preferably Camellia)
3 quarts of water
1 large onion, chopped
2 toes garlic, chopped
4 stalks celery, chopped
1 bell pepper, chopped
1 bunch green onions, chopped (white and green parts)
1 pound beef smoked sausage, sliced
1 pound seasoned ham, or a ham steak, cut into pieces
Creole seasoning to taste
black pepper to taste

Wash peas and put them in large pot with water. Bring to a boil and add onion and garlic. When it comes to a boil again, turn heat down to very low. Let this cook for about an hour, stir occasionally. Then add celery, bell pepper, sausage and ham. Cook on low for several more hours, stir occasionally and add green onions. Add the remaining easonings to taste. To get the smooth consistency, melt a half stick of butter in a separate small pan, add two to three tablespoons of flour and fry this down for about 5 minutes till smooth but not turning brown, stirring constantly. Then turn the beans up to a higher heat and get them boiling real good, add the roux, stir in totally and reduce heat immediately. They should then be the right consistency, but they will begin to stick to the bottom of the pan if not on low heat. Serve with rice of choice.

Black Eyed Peas and Cabbage

It's tradition to serve black eyed peas and cabbage every New Year's Day. As a child I refused to eat either, but my parents bordered on child cruelty by making me eat one pea and a sliver of cabbage every year. They said it was for my own good! You see, black eyed peas bring good luck, and cabbage brings money. This year I had a full serving of both; I needed it!

Panned Pork Chops

4 center cut pork chops
2 eggs beaten
1-2 cups bread crumbs, seasoned
salt and pepper to taste
garlic powder to taste

Trim the pork chops of all fat. Dip in egg and dip in Italian seasoned bread crumbs. Fry in a black iron skillet with a small amount of oil on the bottom. Fry on medium, the coating will burn on high, season to taste, turn over and fry till desired doneness.

Smothered Cabbage

"150 square miles of city destroyed!"

1 onion chopped
1 head cabbage, sliced
1/4 pound smoked ham
1 teaspoon vinegar
1 piece of smoked sausage, diced
1 teaspoon salt
1/2 teaspoon pepper

Sauté onion and meat. Oil can be added if necessary. Add cabbage, Add salt and pepper and vinegar; cover and cook over low heat for about 1 1/2 to 2 hours.

Creole Maque Choux

1 link smoked sausage, diced
1 1/2 cups (2 onions) onion, diced
1 cup yellow pepper, de stemmed, de seeded, and diced
1 cup red pepper, de stemmed, de seeded, and diced
1 jalapeno pepper, de stemmed, de seeded, and diced
2 tablespoons olive oil
1 (10 ounce) package frozen sliced okra, thawed and sliced thin
2 tablespoons garlic, minced
2 cups frozen corn (1 bag) thawed
2 cans Rotel
1 (8 ounce) can tomato sauce
2-3 teaspoons Cajun or Creole seasoning, to taste
1/2 teaspoons salt

In a large non-stick skillet, saute the onion, yellow pepper, red pepper, smoked sausage, and jalapeno in olive oil for 5 minutes or until cooked. Add the okra and garlic, and continue to saute for 5 additional minutes. Add the remaining ingredients and stir well to combine. Cover, reduce the heat to low, and simmer for 20-25 minutes or until the vegetables are tender. Taste and adjust seasonings, if necessary.

Where did they go?

After evacuating the New Orleans area, residents were dispersed all over the country. There were a few places that really stand out to me. According to FEMA, over 17,000 people evacuated to California, almost 5,000 people evacuated to Maryland and over 300 people evacuated to Alaska. And I can only imagine how unhappy the 1,700 people who evacuated to Minnesota were when winter arrived. Hopefully, most will return home to New Orleans.

Cornbread

1 1/2 cups cornmeal
1/2 cup flour
1 tablespoon baking powder
1 teaspoon salt
1/4 cup cane syrup
1 egg, beaten
1 cup milk
4 tablespoons melted shortening

Melt shortening in a cast iron skillet. In a bowl, combine egg, milk, cornmeal, flour, baking powder, salt, and syrup. Mix well. Pour shortening into the mix and stir together. Pour the batter into the skillet and bake in a 400 degree oven for 24 minutes until golden brown.

Nanny's Banana Pudding

4 eggs
4 tablespoons flour
1 1/2 cups of sugar
1 can evaporated milk
whole milk, as needed
2 teaspoons vanilla
1/2 stick butter
1 package vanilla wafers
3 egg whites
As many bananas as you like

Separate 4 eggs. Then beat the yolks. Next add 1 1/2 cups sugar and flour. In a one quart jar (mayonnaise jar), add 1 can of evaporated milk and enough whole milk to equal a quart. Pour mixture into a pot and cook on low heat until thick, stir continuously. Remove from heat and add the 1/2 stick butter and vanilla. Layer vanilla wafers, bananas, and 1/2 of the pudding and repeat. Beat egg whites until peaks form. Top banana pudding with egg whites and brown in oven under broiler for about a minute. Chill and serve.

"This is a recipe that my Nanny always made for me as a child. She knew that Marjorie, my sister and I, loved it, so she would always make it when we would go over there. My grandmother wrote down the recipe because Nanny didn't have a written recipe. The directions aren't clear because the recipe wasn't written to be duplicated. You learned how to make banana pudding by watching Nanny."

Megan

Brandy Milk Punch

2 ounces brandy
1 cup milk
1 teaspoon powdered sugar
grated nutmeg for top

Place brandy, milk and powdered sugar in a shaker. Shake and serve. Sprinkle with grated nutmeg.

Bayona Restaurant
430 Dauphine
New Orleans, LA 70113
504-525-4455
www.bayona.com

Grilled Shrimp with Coriander Sauce and Black Bean Cake

Grilled Shrimp

16 medium to large headless shrimp, peeled and de veined
4 tablespoons olive oil
1/2 teaspoon chopped garlic
1/2 teaspoon ground cumin
1/2 teaspoon ground coriander
1/4 teaspoon cayenne pepper
1/2 teaspoon salt

Toss shrimp with olive oil, garlic, salt, pepper and spices. Skewer 4 to a portion and set aside.

Coriander Sauce

2 tablespoons shallots finely chopped
1 teaspoon orange zest
2 ounces orange juice
4 ounces white wine
2 tablespoons sherry wine vinegar
1 teaspoon ground coriander
6 ounces butter, softened
1 tablespoon cilantro, chopped
salt and pepper to taste

In a small saucepan, place chopped shallots, orange zest, ground coriander, orange juice, wine and vinegar. Simmer over medium heat until liquid is reduced to 2-3 tablespoons. While still hot, whisk in softened butter by the tablespoonful until sauce is thick and creamy. Stir in chopped cilantro and season with salt and pepper to taste. Keep warm, but not hot. Broil or grill shrimp, 2-3 minutes each side until just cooked through. Place with warm coriander sauce and serve with black bean cake.

Black Bean Cake

1 pound black beans
1 green bell pepper, chopped
1 onion, chopped
1 small Jalapeno, chopped
1 tablespoon garlic, minced
2 tablespoons honey
2 tablespoons cider vinegar
1 teaspoon chili powder
1 teaspoon ground cumin
salt
pepper

Cook black beans in water until tender. Saute onion, peppers and garlic over medium heat for 2-3 minutes. Add the beans and other ingredients to the pot. Season with salt and pepper and stir frequently until the beans have absorbed the water and start to break down. Puree and dry. Form beans into cakes and dust with flour. Saute the cakes and serve with a dollop of sour cream and sprig of cilantro.

BEEF
RAVIOLI
ndividual
AmeriQual Packaging Evansville, IN 47710
GOVERNMENT PROPERTY COMMERCIAL RESALE IS UNLAW
LAMELESS RATION HEATERS ARE PROHIBITED ON COMMERCIA
AIRLINES UNLESS SEALED IN ORIGINAL MRE MENU BAG
Peelable Seal
Mea
Ready-to-Eat
MENU NO. 3
BEEF
RAVIOLI
Individual
AmeriQual Packaging Evansville, IN 47710
.S. GOVERNMENT PROPERTY COMMERCIAL RESALE IS UNLAWF

Romantic Dinner for Two or Twenty

Mandina's: Oyster Artichoke Soup

Old English Petit Fours
Shrimp Remoulade Salad
Potato Rockefeller
Beef Tenderloin
Cajun Grilled Ratatouille
Red Velvet Bites
Ramos Gin Fizz
Dawn's Chocolate Martini

Whole Foods: Seared Tuna With Sauteed Greens
Salad of Pomegranates, Green Beans, Jicama and Walnuts

Mandina's Restaurant
3800 Canal Street
New Orleans, LA 70119
504-482-9179
www.mandinas.com

Oyster and Artichoke Soup For a Really Large Crowd!

1 cup bay leaves
1 cup oregano
12 ounces granulated garlic
3 pints chicken base
1/2 gallon oil
1 gallon flour
3 stalks celery, chopped
4 bunch green onions, chopped
4 bunch parsley, chopped
3 large onions, chopped
4 gallons oysters and juice
6 large cans artichoke hearts, drained
2 ounces Tobasco Sauce

After the storm, Mandina's Restaurant decided to keep up with the influx of its customers in the Baton Rouge area. A new location was established:

7655 Old Hammond Hwy.
Baton Rouge, LA 70809

Fill a 20 gallon pot 1/2 full with water and bring to a boil. Add the first four ingredients. Stir and cover. In another pan, create a light roux with oil and flour and stir. Add the next four ingredients to the roux and cook down about 15 minutes. Add roux mixture, oysters, artichokes and Tabasco to the 20 gallon pot. Bring the mixture to a boil and then remove from heat.

Tourism

There is a new kind of tourism emerging in New Orleans and I believe that many will agree it is uncomfortable and sometimes unwelcome. The pre-K tourist visited the French Quarter, fine dining establishments and historic uptown buildings.

The post-K tourist often wants the complete "devastation" tour. Many have good intentions, others just morbid curiosity but either way, it is distressing and sometimes downright rude.

For example, as you know, my home was ten houses from the levee break on the canal; therefore, it was devastation tour central. Lines of cars, complete traffic jams and hundreds of people became part of the "new normal." None of them appeared to be residents of the neighborhood.

One day, a young lady stepped out of a van, walked up and started snapping pictures of me covered in mud attempting to salvage some pieces of my old life. There was no, "Hello. How are you? Can I help?" Only snap, snap, snap of her camera. Maybe she assumed it was like visiting the zoo, and the animals on display had no feelings. Or maybe she was just rude. My husband offered her a shovel and said, "Did you come to help?" At that point, she just walked away.

Shortly after that experience, another van full of people pulled in front of our home. They all jumped out with smiles on their faces: mom, dad, three teenagers and young boy. I thought surely they know something I don't since they look so happy. But that wasn't the case. Instead, they thought it was a great idea to take a family picture in front of a flooded car in the driveway of a flooded home. Oh what fun!

Consequently, we are faced with a struggle. Do we say, "No more tours, leave us alone, enough already?" Or do we say, "Take all of the pictures you want, enjoy our misfortune and put five dollars in the bucket when you leave?"

Old English Petit Fours

3 loaves of Pepperidge Farm sandwich bread
3 1/2 sticks of margarine, room temperature
4 (5 ounce) jars of Kraft Old English Cheese Spread
1 1/2 tablespoons Worcestershire sauce
1 teaspoon Tabasco
1 teaspoon onion powder
dash cayenne
dry dill and paprika to top

Using an electric knife cut all crusts off of the bread. Combine cheese, margarine, Worcestershire, Tabasco, onion powder and cayenne in a food processor. It will appear like an icing. Spread mixture between 3 slices of bread. Cut into 4 triangles and spread mixture on sides and top. Sprinkle with dill, paprika and cayenne if you prefer it spicier. Freeze. When ready to serve, place petit fours on cookie sheet frozen in oven at 350 degrees for 20 minutes or until golden brown. Great for unexpected guests! This is a two bottle of wine project, and many hands are helpful. Have a cooking party just to make this.

Shrimp Remoulade Salad

3/4 cup salad oil
1/4 cup fresh lemon juice
1/4 cup Creole mustard
2 tablespoons horseradish, drained
1/3 cup onion, finely chopped
1/3 cup celery, finely chopped
2 tablespoons green onions
2 tablespoons parsley, finely chopped
2 teaspoons paprika
1 teaspoons salt
1/8 teaspoons pepper
1/8 teaspoons cayenne
1 clove garlic minced
fresh mixed greens

Put all ingredients in the food processor and pulse until blended, about 5 times. Chill and toss shrimp in Remoulade sauce and place over a bed of mixed greens.

Potato Rockefeller

2 boxes frozen spinach, cooked and drained
5 large Yukon gold potatoes
1 cup Asiago and Parmesan blend cheese mix
1 bunch of green onions
1 clove of garlic
1/2 stick butter
1/2 cup heavy cream
5 slices prosciutto, chopped
Crystal Hot Sauce to taste
Pernod (enough to de glaze the pan)

Clean, peel and boil potatoes and place in a large bowl with the cooked spinach. Sauté onions, garlic and prosciutto. De glaze pan with Pernod. Add mixture to bowl with potatoes and spinach. Cream the mixture with hand blender and add butter, cheeses and cream until desired consistency is reached. Add Crystal Hot Sauce to taste. More Pernod can be added if desired. Place in baking dish and cook at 350 degrees until warm throughout, about 15-20 minutes.

Beef Tenderloin

1/4 cup whole grain mustard
1/4 cup Zatarain's Creole mustard
5 tablespoons extra virgin olive oil
2 tablespoons oregano
2 tablespoon marjoram
1 tablespoon dried thyme, finely crumbled
1 whole filet of beef (7 to 8 pound untrimmed or 5 to 6 pound trimmed)
vegetable oil for sautéing
Tony's generously
freshly ground black pepper

In a small bowl, mix together the mustard, olive oil, oregano, thyme and marjoram and make a paste. Cut the filet in half to makes two equal pieces. Heat the oven to 450 degrees. Heat a heavy duty roasting pan or cast iron skillet over medium-high heat. Pour in enough oil to just cover the bottom of the pan. Pat the filet dry, sprinkle Tony's generously, and lay in the pan; cook without disturbing until the bottom is a rich brown. Turn the beef and sear the other sides. It will take about 4 min. per side turning it about four times to get a good sear. When the filets are seared, transfer them to a cutting board, rub them with the mustard and herb mix. Put a rack in the roasting pan, lay the meat on the rack, and roast until the internal temperature reaches 120 degrees for medium rare, about 20 minutes. Remove the filets from the oven and let them rest in a warm spot for at least 15 minutes before slicing.

MRE's (Meals Ready to Eat)

Who said the federal government wasn't prepared for Katrina? Actually, all of the MRE's distributed were "Louisiana Ready." Just about every meal contains a little bottle of Tabasco sauce to make it more palatable. Most people I've met had enough Beef Stew MRE's to last a month, but rumor has it that MRE's also come in Jambalaya and Cajun Rice. Either way, they filled empty tummies and made people appreciative of a home cooked meal where Tabasco is a condiment, not a main ingredient.

Cajun Grilled Ratatouille

3 cloves garlic
3/4 cup olive oil
3 yellow squash
3 zucchini
2 eggplants
3 bell peppers- yellow, red and orange
1 pack white mushrooms
2 tomatoes
1 onion
1 tablespoon sweet basil
1 tablespoon Creole seasoning
2 bay leaves
1/2 cup chicken stock
1 bottle Italian salad dressing

Slice zucchini into 1/2 inch pieces. Cut peppers into 1/4 inch strips, slice onions thinly, cut yellow squash into circles, cut and peel eggplant into 1 inch cubes and peel and quarter tomatoes, peel garlic. Place the above vegetables and pack of mushrooms into a large Ziploc bag and marinate overnight in basil, bay leaves, chicken stock and salad dressing. Place drained and marinated vegetables in a grill basket, sprinkle with Creole seasoning and cook on barbecue pit on medium heat until done, about 20 minutes.

It can happen to you!

Catastrophe is not limited to the Gulf Coast. According to the Insurance Center Associates, only one in five California homeowners carries earthquake insurance. There is an 86 percent chance of a catastrophic (magnitude 7 or stronger) earthquake occurring in California within 20 years, according to a January 1995 report by the scientists at the University of California. A catastrophic earthquake striking Los Angeles or San Francisco could cause insured damage of $100 billion. New studies project higher losses from future hurricanes: $53 billion for a class five hurricane striking Miami, and $51 billion for a class four storm striking New Jersey and Long Island.

Red Velvet Bites

1 box red velvet cake mix
1 container cream cheese frosting
1 bag white chocolate chips

Bake the cake according to package directions. Cool and crumble the cake with your hands. Stir in cream cheese frosting and roll into 1 inch balls. Freeze balls on a wax paper lined pan and then dip in melted white chocolate. Refrigerate and serve at room temperature.

Ramos Gin Fizz

1 bar spoon powdered sugar
3 dashes orange flower water
1/2 ounce fresh lemon juice
1/4 ounce fresh lime juice
1/2 ounce egg white
1 ounce gin
2 1/4 ounces milk

Fill a shaker a 1/3 with ice. Add the ingredients in the order listed above. Cover and shake until the mixture is creamy and foamy. Strain into a tall glass and serve.

Dawn's Chocolate Martini

1 1/2 ounce vanilla vodka
1 ounce Godiva Chocolate Liqueur
1 shot Bailey's
1 shot half and half
Hershey's chocolate syrup for garnish

Pour all ingredients into martini shaker, except chocolate syrup. Shake with ice until well blended and cold.
Zigzag Hershey's on martini glasses. Pour mixture into glasses and serve.

The Saints Game at Tiger Stadium

Many Saints season ticket holders were certain that the long lines at the ticket office were a result of intentional attempts to lose support and move the team to San Antonio after hurricane Katrina. During a time when residents were stressed to the max, the football game was expected to be a welcome respite. Unfortunately, the visit to LSU was chaotic, disorganized and tense. As loyal season ticket holders, we were unable to enter the stadium, for the first Saints game in Tiger Stadium, until halftime because of the lines and disorganization. Once there, most fans really needed a beer and until weeks before the game Tiger Stadium was not equipped with beer booths, beer guys or anything beer related. Baton Rouge officials made exceptions for the influx of New Orleanians and stocked the college stadium with the football watching necessities. Most New Orleanians take for granted the fact that beer can be purchased on Sundays and that "go cups" actually exist. I can only imagine how angry the mobs would have been after waiting until halftime to enter only to find no beer.

Seared Tuna with Sautéed Greens

Whole Foods Market
3400 Veterans Highway
Metairie, LA
504-888-8225
www.wholefoods.com

4 tuna steaks (11/2 pounds total)
4 tablespoons olive oil
1 small onion, finely chopped
2 garlic cloves, finely chopped
1 (14 ounce) can diced tomatoes
1 bunch Swiss chard (red or white), stems removed then washed and chopped
salt and freshly ground black pepper

Marinade
3/4 cup orange juice
1 tablespoon fresh thyme, finely chopped
2 tablespoon extra virgin olive oil

Marinate tuna steaks in orange juice, thyme, and 2 tablespoons of the olive oil for 30 minutes. While the tuna is marinating, sauté onion and garlic in 2 tablespoons olive oil over low to medium heat until softened. Add tomatoes and simmer for 5 minutes. Add chard, cover and cook for 5 to 8 minutes more or until greens are bright green and tender. Season with salt and pepper and set aside. In a large sauté pan, heat the remaining 2 tablespoons of olive oil. When the oil is hot, season the tuna with lots of freshly ground black pepper then sear the tuna for 3-5 minutes of each side for medium-rare. Remove tuna steaks, add marinating liquid and reduce for 3-5 minutes. Serve tuna atop a serving of greens, drizzle with marinade.

"Packed with good nutrition and loaded with flavor, this recipe is a boost for your body and taste buds courtesy of Whole Foods Market."

Whole Foods

Whole Foods Company began in New Orleans in 1974 in a small corner shop in Uptown New Orleans. The first location was in a cooperative natural foods market. Within a few years, a new store was added in the Bayou St. John neighborhood on Esplanade Avenue. Just three months after opening the Veterans store, Hurricane Katrina struck, devastating New Orleans. Though there was uncertainty after the storm, Whole Foods Market stood by the people of New Orleans. Its leadership gave eleven pallets of food to the Gumbo Krewe so they could prepare meals for the first responders. Additionally the store officials authorized a New Orleans policeman to "open" the uptown store to anyone needing supplies. At the time of the hurricane, the two stores in New Orleans, Uptown and Metairie, employeed a few hundred team members. Remarkably, the company took great steps to guarantee employees pay through the end of September, gave them relocation funds and guaranteed them a job anywhere there was a Whole Foods Market in the country. The store has decided New Orleans is a city with a historic past and a stellar future, and Whole Foods Market wants to be a part of that future. We continue to welcome them as a member of the community

Salad of Pomegranates, Green Beans, Jicama and Walnuts

1 1/2 pomegranates
1 medium jicama
1 pound green beans
1/4 cup walnuts
1 tablespoon chopped fresh flat-leafed, Italian Parsley
1 tablespoon extra virgin olive oil
1 tablespoon fresh lemon juice

Without cutting the pomegranate, roll fruit on counter top to burst interior seeds. When "popping" has stopped, carefully pierce fruit with a knife or ice pick and squeeze out juice, you need 1/4 cup. Peel and cut jicama into 1/4 inch slices. On a cutting board stack slices, 2 or 3 at a time, and cut into 1/4 inch-thick sticks. In a bowl, toss jicama with pomegranate juice. Chill mixture, covered, tossing occasionally, 30 minutes to allow jicama to absorb some of the juice. Have a bowl of ice and cold water ready. Trim green beans, and in a saucepan of boiling salted water, blanch for two minutes, or until crisp and tender. Transfer beans with a slotted spoon to ice water to stop cooking and drain in a colander. Cut remaining pomegranate in half with hands by gently breaking it into two. Bend back rinds and dislodge seeds from membranes. Coarsely chop walnuts. To jicama mixture add beans, pomegranate seeds, parsley, oil, lemon juice, and salt and pepper to taste. Toss to combine. Serve salad sprinkled with walnuts.

Parade Route

Mrs. Fannie's Fried Chicken
Mother's Club Jambalaya
Cajun Fire and Ice Pickles
King Cake
Muffulettas on Danno's Muffuletta Bread
George's Bloody Mary

Lilette:
Duck Confit with Savory Spinach
and Mushroom Vinaigrette

You can tell a Y'at!

You really can pick out a "Y'at" a mile away! They don't always blend into their surroundings, and their loud, accented voices often permeate a room. And the sound of a familiar "Dawlin" is welcoming and beloved by all who understand it.

When Denice and Billy were on their honeymoon in Scotland, they were forced to wait hours in the airport. Denice looked around and witnessed a lady in a Viking hat with two gold yarn braids talking with everyone around her. Denice began to think, "We're not in Minnesota, and this is not Norway, and I swear that woman just *axed* a question." She turned to her husband and said, "I think that lady is from New Orleans. In fact, I know that lady is from New Orleans."

Billy seriously doubted that the wildly dressed stranger was from New Orleans, but he made a deal with his new wife. Billy offered to walk past the woman on the way to the men's room to better assess her accent. Since he was wearing an LSU golf shirt, he figured that only a Louisiana native would stop him to chat. What do you know? She stopped him with a very loud, cheery "Dawlin, Where y'at? You from elesshoo?"

After a very pleasant conversation, they all parted ways, and Denice said to her new husband, "Even on vacation, my people think every day is Mardi Gras." They still don't know why the friendly stranger was wearing a Viking hat!

The Katrina and Rita X

A large X was placed on each home searched after Katrina. The top quadrant included the date and the bottom, the number of bodies found. Even seven months after the storm, these X's are everywhere. It seems impossible to erase these horrific markings from our homes and our minds.

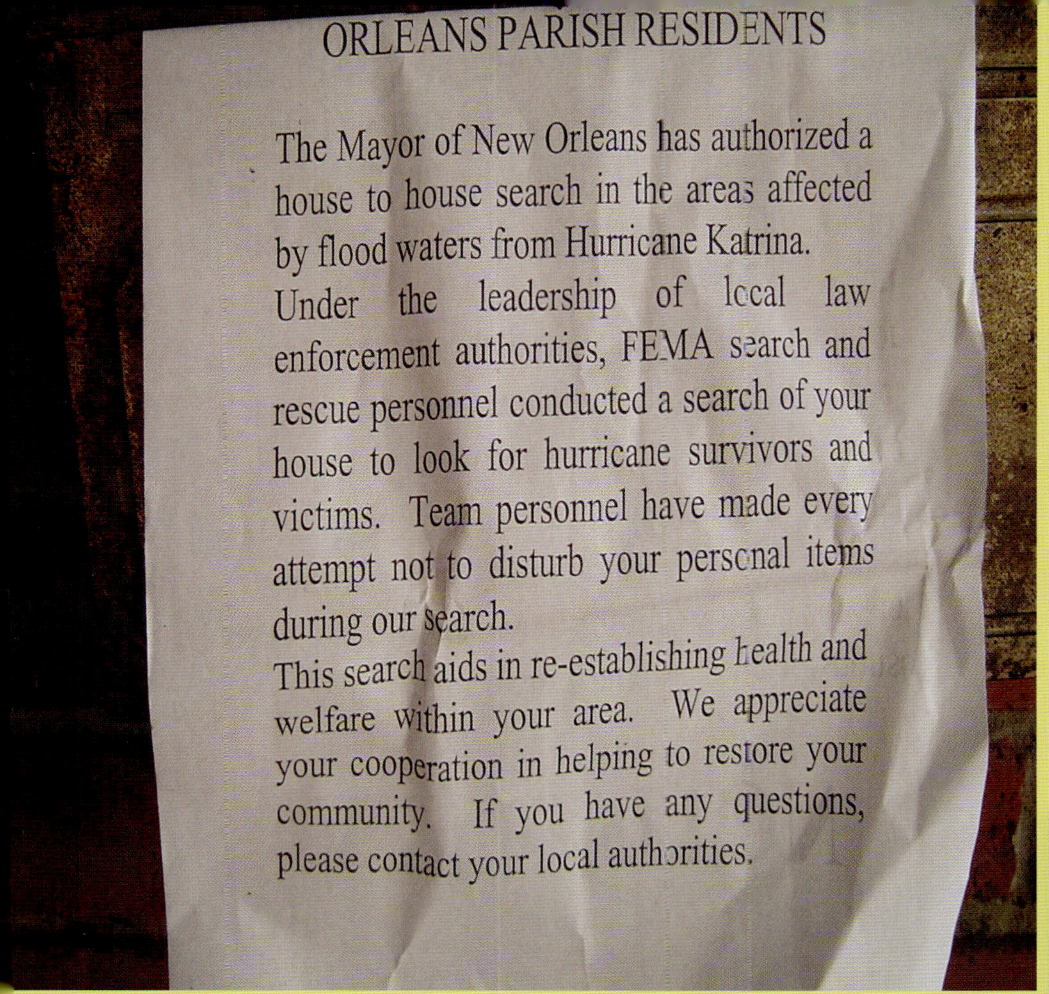
ORLEANS PARISH RESIDENTS
The Mayor of New Orleans has authorized a house to house search in the areas affected by flood waters from Hurricane Katrina.
Under the leadership of local law enforcement authorities, FEMA search and rescue personnel conducted a search of your house to look for hurricane survivors and victims. Team personnel have made every attempt not to disturb your personal items during our search.
This search aids in re-establishing health and welfare within your area. We appreciate your cooperation in helping to restore your community. If you have any questions, please contact your local authorities.

THE CHURCH OF GOD
WELCOMES ALL PEOPLE

Mrs. Fannie's Fried Chicken

20 pieces chicken
6 cups all purpose flour
salt
pepper
cayenne
paprika
1 bottle Crisco oil

Sprinkle chicken with paprika, black pepper, salt and cayenne if you want spicy chicken. Lightly coat chicken in flour and set aside to rest for thirty minutes. Sprinkle again with seasoning and dredge a second time in flour. This forms a good crust. Fry in oil on medium heat. Cover for the first 3-5 minutes. Lift cover and fry until golden brown or juices run clear when pierced with a fork. Set in 250 degrees oven until the remainder of the chicken is finished.

"This is a simple jambalaya recipe that's easy and fail-proof. The Mother's Club at St. Pius makes this dish for the Teacher Appreciation luncheon once a year. When they all learned how easy it was, it became a staple for family dinners and large gatherings." Claire

Mother's Club Jambalaya

1 pound smoked sausage
1 (8 ounce) can of tomato sauce
2 cups of raw rice
1/4 cup of shallots
1 can of beef broth
1 can of French onion soup
1 stick of margarine
parsley and thyme to taste

Mix all ingredients together and put in 350 degree oven for 1 1/2 hours in a covered heavy pot.

Cajun Fire and Ice Pickles

2 (46 ounce) jars whole dill pickles
4 cups sugar
2 tablespoons Crystal Hot Sauce
1/2 to 1/4 teaspoons crushed pepper
3 cloves garlic

Slice pickles in half long way. Mix 1/2 of the olive juice, sugar, hot sauce, garlic and red peppers in a Ziploc bag. Shake well. Refrigerate and let stand for two hours. Turn occasionally. Pack the bag in your ice chest for the parade route!

King Cake

1/2 cup warm water (115°F)
2 packages active dry yeast
1/2 cup plus 2 teaspoons sugar, in all
3 1/2 to 4 1/2 cups flour, unsifted
1 teaspoon nutmeg
2 teaspoons salt
1 teaspoon lemon zest (grated lemon rind)
1/2 cup warm milk
5 egg yolks
1 stick butter cut into slices and softened, plus 2 tablespoons more softened butter
1 egg slightly beaten with 1 tablespoon milk
1 teaspoon cinnamon
Egg wash
1 one-inch plastic baby doll (or bean)

Icing
3 cups powdered sugar
1/4 cup lemon juice
3 to 6 tablespoons water

Talent

It takes talent, planning and patience to be a successful parade-goer. Year after year family members return to the same location to watch Mardi Gras parades. They stake out the perfect spot early in the day and pack a full buffet of food and drinks while setting up the family ladder for a perfect view. The talent is necessary when the parade starts. Only a Mardi Gras veteran can catch beads, hold a beer and make sure the kids don't fall off of the ladder all at the same time!

Pour warm water into a small, bowl. Sprinkle yeast and 2 teaspoons of sugar on water surface and allow the mixture to rest for three minutes. Then mix thoroughly. Set bowl in a warm area until yeast bubbles and the mixture almost doubles in volume. In another bowl, combine 3 1/2 cups of flour, remaining sugar, nutmeg and salt. Sift into a large mixing bowl. Stir in lemon zest. Make a hole in the center of the mixture and pour in the yeast mix and milk. Add egg yolks. Using a wooden spoon, slowly combine dry ingredients into the yeast and milk mixture. When mixture is smooth, beat in 8 tablespoons butter adding it one at a time. Continue to beat for 2 minutes, or until dough can be shaped into a ball. Place ball of dough on a lightly floured surface and knead like bread. While kneading, sprinkle up to 1 cup more of flour one tablespoon at a time over the dough. The dough will begin to feel dry and less sticky. Keep kneading for about ten minutes until it is shiny. Brush the dough with softened butter. Cover and allow to rise for over an hour. It should be double the size after rising. Remove dough from bowl and place on lightly floured surface and punch it down. Sprinkle cinnamon over the top, pat and shape the dough into long strands. Create a twist or a braid and create a circle. Place on a buttered baking sheet and let rest for an hour or until it doubles in size again. Brush the cake with egg was and bake in a 375 degree oven for 30 minutes until golden brown. Cool and add bean or plastic baby in the cake at this time. To make the icing, combine sugar, lemon juice and 3 tablespoons of water until smooth. If icing is too stiff, add more water. Spread the icing over the top of cake and immediately sprinkle with colored sugars (purple, green and gold.)

Danno's Muffuletta Bread

1 cup warm water (110 degrees)
1 tablespoon active dry yeast
1 tablespoon granulated sugar
2 cups all purpose flour
1 cup bread flour
1 1/2 teaspoons iodized salt
2 tablespoons lard or vegetable shortening
sesame seeds
3 tablespoons extra virgin olive oil

Egg Wash:
1 egg
2 tablespoons cold water

Combine the water, yeast and sugar in the work bowl of a stand mixer, stir well and let stand for 5-10 minutes or until good and foamy. Meanwhile, combine the flours, salt, and lard in a bowl and work in the fat with your hands until broken up into very small pieces. When the yeast is foamy, fit the mixer with a dough hook attachment and gradually add the flour on low speed until its all incorporated. Scrape the sides down between additions. When the dough comes together, turn it onto a floured work surface and knead until smooth and elastic, 5-10 minutes, adding more flour if necessary. Alternatively, you can let the machine do the work, but for me, bread is a touch thing. Coat a large bowl with the olive oil, then put the dough in, turning once to coat both sides. Cover loosely with a clean dry towel, or plastic wrap. Let the dough rise in a warm place until doubled in bulk, about 1-1/2 hours. Punch the dough down and shape into a flat round about 9 inches across (It will expand to about 10″.) Place the dough on a lightly oiled baking sheet. Sprinkle the top with sesame seeds, about 2-3 tablespoons should do it, then press them lightly into the dough. Loosely cover the loaf and let rise until doubled in bulk, about 1 hour. When the dough has risen, remove the cover, gently brush with the egg wash then gently place into a preheated 425 degree oven for 10 minutes. Turn the heat down to 375 degrees for an additional 25 minutes or until it's golden brown and sounds hollow when tapped.

"The good news about wearing other people's clothes, they're already broken in and comfy."

Muffulettas

1 jar Boscoli Olive Salad with oil
1 round loaf Italian bread
1/4 pound mortadella, thinly sliced
1/4 pound ham, thinly sliced
1/4 pound hard Genoa salami, thinly sliced
1/4 pound Mozzarella cheese, sliced
1/4 pound Provolone cheese, sliced

Cut an (muffuletta) Italian loaf horizontally. Spread each half with equal parts of olive salad and oil. Layer the remaining ingredients and cut in quarters. Enjoy!

Leftover Olive Salad?

Mix it with 6 ounces of feta cheese, 4 tablespoons olive oil and 1-2 tablespoons balsamic vinegar. Serve over mixed greens as a tangy salad dressing.

George's Famous Bloody Mary

1 bottle Major Peters Blood Mary Mix
2 squeezed lemons
2 squeezed limes
3 tablespoons of Worcestershire sauce
1 tablespoon celery salt
1 tablespoon lemon pepper
1 tablespoon Louisiana Red Hot Sauce
1 shot vodka per glass

Combine all ingredients except vodka, stir well and chill. Add vodka immediately before serving. Serve over ice and garnish.

Lilette Restaurant
3637 Magazine Street
New Orleans, LA 70115
504-895-1636
www.liletterestaurant.com

Duck Confit with Savory Spinach and Mushroom Vinaigrette

1 gallon rendered duck fat
12 Muscovy or Mouland duck legs
1 cup kosher salt
1/4 cup Herbs de Provence
1 pack savoy spinach
1/2 gallon of assorted mushrooms (Crimini, Oyster, Shitake)
1/3 cup white balsamic vinegar
1/3 cup sherry vinegar
1 tablespoon fresh thyme, chopped
1 tablespoon chopped garlic
1 cup extra virgin olive oil
1 tablespoon Dijon mustard

Cure duck legs by mixing together Kosher salt and Herbs de Provence. Sprinkle on both sides of duck liberally (Confit should be salty). Let sit for 24 hours. Melt duck fat into a casserole or hotel pan that will accommodate 12 duck legs in one layer. Submerge duck legs. Fat must cover duck legs completely. Place in 300 degree oven for about 2 1/2 hours until thighbone is easily removed. Ducks may be held in fat for up to one month. Sauté all mushrooms (separately) in vegetable oil. Season well. Cool and chop finely. Put mushrooms in a bowl. Add all remaining ingredients. The vinaigrette should be broken (not emulsified).

Remember: all vinaigrette recipes are not set in stone. Adjust vinegar and oil amounts if necessary.

To Serve:

Pull duck legs from fat and crisp in a non-stick pan. Heat through in oven. Toss spinach with the mushroom vinaigrette and serve confit on top.

Mardi Gras

This year was the 150th anniversary of Mardi Gras. How can you not celebrate something that has happened for 150 years? More than ever, this year I needed a party, a reason to celebrate and a reason to gather with friends. This year's celebration was one of the best ever. It was about masked men nd women throwing trinkets while riding ornately decorated satirical floats. It was about gathering with old friends and new acquaintances. It was about catching up and sharing stories while enjoying the show. Mardi Gras was about children dancing to marching bands and people in costumes poking fun at their own personal situation. Mardi Gras was about showing the world what New Orleans has to offer while showing how far we have to go. It was about family, fun, music and tradition.

HEADLESS SHRIMP
10-15 Count $9.95 Per-Pound

Repent It's Lent

Reneetouffe

Julie's Shrimp Creole

Shrimp Chowder a la Marianne

Seafood Fettucinni

BBQ Shrimp

Hot Oyster Dip

Seafood Casserole

Crabmeat Au Gratin

Peristyle:

Asparagus Soup

Dog Gumbo?

Immediately after hurricane Katrina passed, Bob was back on the office phone conducting business with customers on the west coast. He didn't realize how bad things were in other parts of the city.

Before the storm, Aunt Ruth had called from Jackson and recommended he place two axes in the attic. Luckily, he didn't need them. However, Bob soon realized life in New Orleans after Katrina was not the same as with other recent storms. The power was out, and looters were beginning to take over the streets in his area.

He remained in contact with friends and family who evacuated for the storm and knew that their return in the near future was not possible. He began placing signs to deter looters, cleaning out freezers and taking note of property damage. Many of his friends rewarded his efforts by offering him the contents of their wine cellars.

After a long day of helping his friends, Bob returned home for dinner. With the findings from his neighbors' freezers and surplus of fine wine, Bob was able to host a party every evening for the remaining residents and rescue workers. Each night, the crowd grew larger and people began arriving with their own offerings of food and wine to share. The attendees dined by candlelight and discussed the challenges ahead.

As the days went on, Bob's signs in the neighborhood became famous. The signs truly deterred the looters while entertaining area residents.

Upon seeing one of Bob's homemade signs, you may ask yourself, "What exactly is dog gumbo?" One foreign journalist asked Bob the same thing, and then asked for his recipe. After making up an incredibly sarcastic story about how to make a pot of dog gumbo, Bob gave her a recipe. Unfortunately, with the language barrier, the journalist didn't quite understand that Bob was being facetious. She eagerly wrote down every word of their conversation.

Days later, Bob received a phone call from a producer verifying the story before it was made public. The producer asked Bob if the recipe he provided was accurate. Bob couldn't help but snicker, "She didn't get it, did she?" You see, the producer understood Bob was full of it and knew the conversation explaining the situation with the journalist would be difficult!

But surely you can understand the journalist's point of view. Why wouldn't she assume people from Louisiana eat just about anything, even dog gumbo? Think about it, We eat alligator, rabbit, nutria, crawfish, and even sweetbreads.

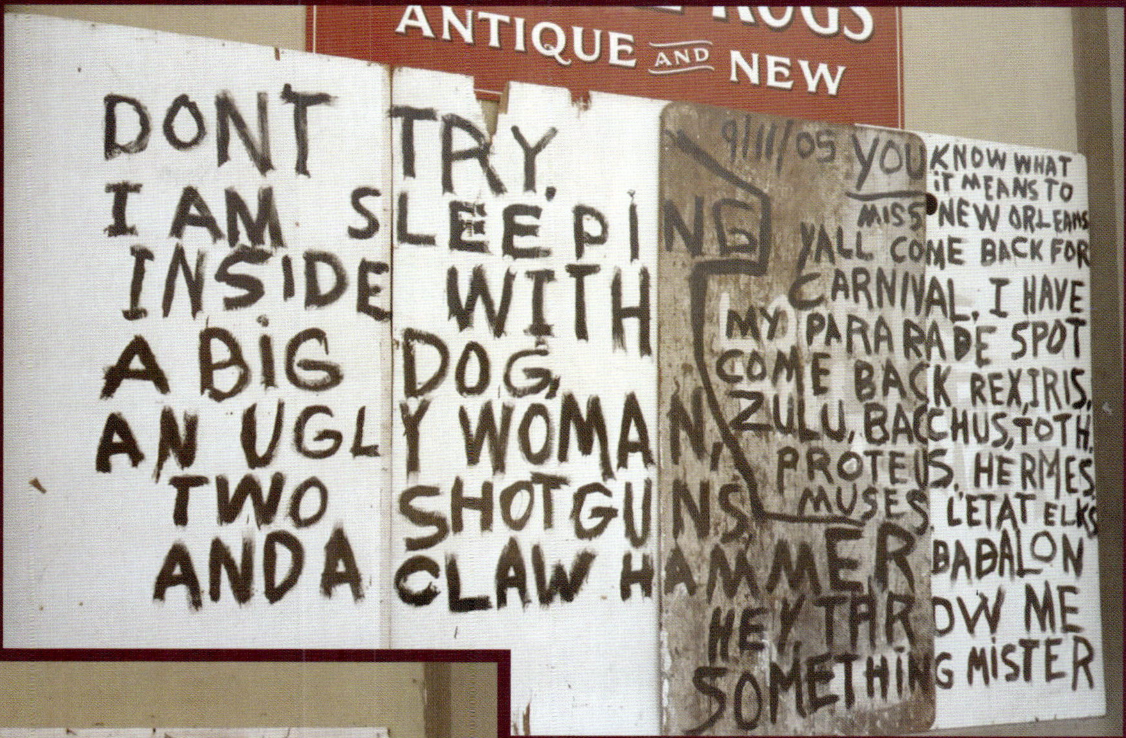
ANTIQUE AND NEW
DONT TRY.
I AM SLEEPING
INSIDE WITH
A BIG DOG,
AN UGLY WOMAN,
TWO SHOTGUNS,
AND A CLAW HAMMER
9/11/05 YOU KNOW WHAT IT MEANS TO MISS NEW ORLEANS
YALL COME BACK FOR CARNIVAL. I HAVE MY PARARADE SPOT
COME BACK REX, IRIS, ZULU, BACCHUS, TOTH, PROTEUS, HERMES, MUSES, L'ETAT, ELKS
BABALON
HEY THROW ME SOMETHING MISTER

9/4/05
STILL HERE
WOMAN
LEFT FRI.
COOKING
A POT OF
DOG
GUMBO

WELCOME
9/24 BACK
Y'ALL
GRIN
AND
BEAR
IT

Reneetouffe

1 stick of butter
3/4 cup celery, chopped
3/4 cup onion, chopped
1/4 cup red, yellow or green bell pepper, chopped
1 tablespoon parsley
1 pound crawfish tails
1 bay leaf
1 tablespoon tomato sauce
1 tablespoon lemon juice
1 teaspoon cornstarch to thicken

Sauté celery, onion, bell pepper and parsley in butter. Add crawfish and simmer. Add 1 bay leaf. Add 1 tablespoon of tomato sauce or more if desired. Add splash of lemon. Use cornstarch to thicken if necessary. Remove bay leaf before serving. Serve over rice.

You can identify

Please don't stereotype the New Orleans citizens based on television images, newspaper articles or stories you've heard. Even nine months after the storm and no matter your background, race, income, religion, gender or age, there is someone like you in New Orleans who is still without a home: families, businessmen, teachers, laborers and doctors.

Julie's Shrimp Creole

2 tablespoon oil, olive or vegetable
1/2 chopped onion, medium
1/2 chopped green pepper, medium
1 rib celery, chopped
2 bay leaves
1/4 teaspoon thyme
1 clove garlic
1 (32 ounce) can diced tomatoes
1 pound cleaned shrimp
3-4 tablespoons sherry
2 cups cooked rice

Sauté onion, celery and pepper in oil, add garlic, herbs and tomatoes. Cook 10-20 minutes. Add shrimp and sherry and cook another 3-5 minutes until shrimp are pink. Serve with rice.

Shrimp Chowder a la Marianne

1 pound shrimp (or crawfish)
1 stick of butter
1 bunch of green onions
2 cans cream of potato soup
1 can whole kernel corn (drained)
1 (8 ounce) cream cheese
1 pint half and half (or whipping cream)
1/4 teaspoon crab boil

Sauté shrimp, butter and green onions, then add the remaining ingredients. Heat until completely warmed.

Seafood Fettuccini

1 box of fettuccini noodles
1 (8 ounce) Philadelphia cream cheese
1 bunch of green onions
1 small whipping cream
1 pint half and half
1 tablespoon liquid crab boil
1 can of chicken stock
Romano and Parmesan cheese
1 cup crabmeat or crawfish
1 teaspoon minced garlic

Saute green onions and garlic, then melt cream cheese and butter into the mixture. Add chicken broth and cook down for 30 minutes. Add crab boil. Add whipping cream, half and half, Parmesan and Romano cheese. Sauce will stick to pot when cheese is added. Add crabmeat or crawfish. Serve over cooked fettuccini noodles.

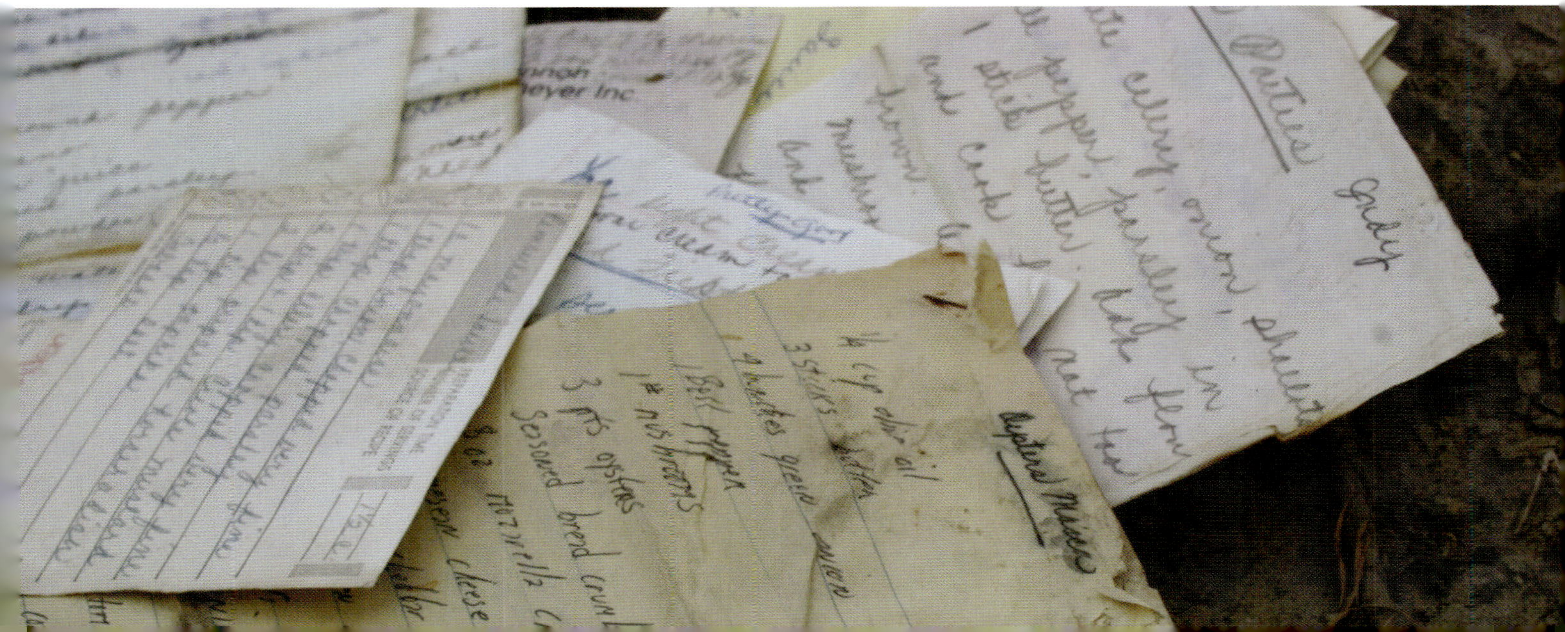

BBQ Shrimp

2 sticks butter, melted
1/2 cup olive oil
4 tablespoons garlic, minced
1 tablespoon black pepper
1 teaspoon Tabasco
4 tablespoons Worcestershire
1 cup chopped fresh basil
1 teaspoon thyme
2-3 pounds jumbo shrimp in shell (unpeeled)

Mix the first 8 ingredients. Cook sauce 4-5 minutes. Place shrimp in individual baking dishes or one large dish. Pour or spoon sauce on top of shrimp. Bake at 350 degrees for 20-30 minutes. Do not overcook. Serve with French bread for dipping. If you use smaller shrimp, bake 5-10 minutes.

Hot Oyster Dip

"This is a secret recipe that my mother-in-law shared only with me. Don't give it to anyone!" Amy

1/4 cup olive
3 sticks butter
4 bunches green onions
1 bell pepper
1 pound of mushrooms
3 pints oysters
1 cup seasoned bread crumbs or more if needed
8 ounces mozzarella cheese
1/2 cup Parmesan cheese
1 can cheddar cheese soup
2 tablespoons garlic powder
1 teaspoon basil
1 bay leaf
1 teaspoon Italian seasonings
hot sauce to taste
1 cup white wine
1 can golden mushroom soup

Spray bottom of large iron pot with vegetable spray. Melt butter in olive oil and add onions and peppers finely chopped. Saute over medium heat until onions are clear. Stir in soups. Drain water from oysters and cut oysters in half unless they are very small. Add to the pot. Stir in seasonings, garlic powder, bay leaf, basil and Italian seasoning and 6 drops of hot sauce. Add white wine and slowly add seasoned bread crumbs. You want a mixture that is like loose grits. Place in a 350 degree oven for thirty minutes. Stir in mozzarella cheese and sprinkle the top with Parmesan. Cover and let sit for ten minutes.

Seafood Casserole

1/2 cup flour
1 stick butter
1 can evaporated milk
1/4 cup celery, chopped
2 onions, chopped
1 red, yellow or green
bell pepper, chopped
1 can sliced mushrooms
1 pound crabmeat
1/2 pound crawfish tails
1 pound shrimp
1/2 pound cheese grated
(your choice)
bread crumbs
salt and pepper to taste

Cook flour, butter and milk into a white sauce. In another pan, sauté celery, onions, bell pepper and mushrooms. Add crabmeat, crawfish and shrimp. Cook through for about ten minutes. Add to the white sauce. If too thick add more milk. Put in casserole dish and top with bread crumbs and cheese. Bake 350 degrees for 25 minutes.

Crabmeat Au Gratin

1 stalk celery, finely chopped
1 cup onion, finely chopped
1/4 pound butter
1/2 cup flour
1 (13 ounce) can evaporated milk
2 egg yolks
1 teaspoon salt
1/4 teaspoon cayenne pepper
1/4 teaspoon black pepper
1 pound white crabmeat
1/2 pound grated American cheese

Saute onion and celery in butter until wilted. Blend flour into the mixture well. Pour milk in gradually while stirring constantly. Add egg yolks, salt, red pepper, black pepper, cook for five minutes. Put crabmeat in a bowl suitable for mixing and pour the cooked sauce over the crabmeat. Blend well and then transfer into a lightly greased casserole dish and sprinkle in grated American cheese. Bake at 375 degrees for 10-15 minutes until light brown.

Peristyle Restaurant
1041 Dumaine Street
New Orleans, LA 70116
504-593-9535
www.wolfesofneworleans.com

Asparagus Soup

1/4 cup butter
1/4 cup all purpose flour
1/2 medium onion with stem in place
3 whole cloves studded in onion*
2 bay leaves
4 cups whole milk
1/4 teaspoon freshly grated nutmeg
6 cups blanched asparagus
Kosher salt to taste
ground white pepper to taste
1 1/2 teaspoons patis**

In three quart sauce pan melt butter and whisk in flour until smooth. Cook constantly, stirring for 3 or 4 minutes without turning the color darker. Then, whisk in milk and bring to a boil, occasionally whisking. Add clove-studded onion, bay leaves and nutmeg and reduce heat to simmer. Cook for 10-15 minutes until the flour is cooked out. If you need to add more milk to maintain consistency, do so carefully to avoid compromising the mixture. The flour must be completely cooked out. Season with salt and pepper and remove from fire. Add blanched asparagus and patis. Pure the soup and strain. Cool in an ice bath.

*clove studded onion: poke holes in the side of an onion with a toothpick about 1/2 inch apart, push the stem end of the clove into each hole

**patis- licorice flavored liqueur

Trailers

I finally got a good laugh after Katrina when I heard a parish official speak of the yearning for FEMA trailers. During a very important, high profile and serious press conference about FEMA, the rebuilding efforts and housing, this official shared his views on trailers. He let the world know that trailers aren't just for "trash" anymore. "Dem rich boys even want trailers." Maybe he wasn't the most eloquent speaker in the world, but he was right in one respect. Everyone wants a trailer, and when they get one, they show it off, they decorate it and they bask in the glory of owning a white aluminum box. Who would have guessed that thousands of homeowners would fight so hard for a lawn ornament that doubles as home? Did ya get yours yet? We're still waiting...

Pray for Us

When the Saints go Marching in

Audrey's Stuffed Artichokes
Anchovy Gravy
Mimi Mary's Meat Sauce
Danno's Corned Beef
Aunt Verlyn's Cabbage Casserole
Irish Coffee

Angelo Brocato:
Italian Sesame Seed Cookies
Italian Fig Cookies

The Rescue Team

Tom and his co-pilot Ardie originally set out to New Orleans from Louisville, KY for what could have been a business opportunity. As helicopter pilots, they both assumed insurance companies would need someone to survey roof damage after the storm had passed. Little did they know, they were in for a life-changing situation.

The day after hurricane Katrina hit, the two gentlemen arrived in Houma, LA and began discussions with family and friends to check on loved ones. They assumed that would keep them busy for a few days. Unbelievably, they were met not only with overwhelming adversity but also with the intense struggle of the people of New Orleans!

The massive scope of the devastation and the limited access to help stranded residents made Tom and his co-pilot a valuable asset to area residents. The two set out to fly rescue missions, escort a national photographer and to offer as much assistance as possible. They dropped water to families trapped on rooftops, picked up men and women stranded on overpasses and reached people who could not be accessed by boats. They transported critical medical patients and delivered fruit and water to anyone they could find.

The two were moved by the courage of the New Orleanians. Men, women and children were trapped on the tops of homes, industrial buildings and schoolhouses. Tom and Ardie both note that regular citizens are not trained on "how to be saved."

Think about how you would feel if everything you've ever known was now under water, you didn't know how to swim, you were afraid of heights, you may have been separated from your family and had no food or water. Or what if you were pregnant, elderly or were very ill? Then think about how you would react if a helicopter dangling a basket arrived to save you, and someone suggested that you climb in with only a small plastic bag filled with a couple of items you could salvage from your flooded life. I don't know about you, but I might be a little reluctant to dangle high above nothing but water in a fragile condition too.

How heroic is one to do what they most fear? Climbing into that basket during such a high-stress situation probably took more courage, bravery and heroism than any of the residents could have imagined they had inside. That strength and will inspired Tom and his co-pilot to keep going through the tough times and continue to save more lives.

There is no telling how many people Tom and Ardie rescued during their days after the storm, but they weren't keeping track. All they cared about was waking up the next morning, after a night sleeping on the floor of an airplane hanger and doing it all over again. They knew in their hearts that this rescue operation was so large and had so many obstacles, every minute and every bit of effort was what they needed to give.

Audrey's Stuffed Artichokes

In a blender chop:
1 large onion
1 head of garlic
2 cans artichoke hearts
1 eight to ten ounce pack of sliced ham
anchovy paste to taste (optional)
4-5 artichokes

Add and blend:
1 "medium" sized can of grated Romano cheese
1/2 can of Parmesan cheese
1 cup Italian style bread crumbs

Place this mixture in a bowl and drizzle with olive oil, stir, continue to add olive oil until "it all holds together." Cut the top off of the artichoke and trim the leaf tips. Stuff the artichokes, wrap in foil, and steam for 1 to 1 1/2 hours or until leaves pull easily from heart.

St. Joseph's Altars

Sicilian immigrants, in honor of the feast of St. Joseph, started St. Joseph's altars. Since ancient times they have celebrated this feast to prevent famine and drought. These altars are prepared for the feast day on March 19th and are often an opportunity for the rich to share with the poor. They show their gratitude to St. Joseph for interceding to God for successful crops. The food on the altar has many biblical references including the Holy Trinity and the Holy Family and is beautifully presented. Fava beans are also associated with the altars because the fava bean thrived in Sicily during severe famines. It is commonly called the "lucky bean." A person who carries a lucky bean will never be without coins.

Anchovy Gravy

1 head of garlic
4 tablespoons oil
3 cans flat anchovies
4 cans tomato paste
1 tomato paste can full red wine
2-3 cans water
1 bay leaf
Italian seasoning to taste
2 cups toasted bread crumbs

Peel garlic and place the pods in foil and drizzle with olive oil. Crimp the foil around the garlic to seal it. Roast the garlic for 10-15 minutes in a 350 degree oven, or until the garlic is soft. Over medium heat, place garlic and excess oil in a medium pot with the anchovies. While cooking the garlic and anchovies, create a paste. Add the tomato paste, red wine, bay leaf, Italian seasoning and water. Make sure the sauce is thick, but not too thick. Add water as necessary. Reduce heat to low and stir as needed. Serve over pasta and top with toasted bread crumbs.

Mimi Mary's Meat Sauce

3 tablespoons olive oil
1 garlic
1 onion
1 bell pepper
1 pound ground meat
2-3 tablespoons sugar
2-3 pinches baking soda
1 package sliced mushrooms
2 cans tomato paste
1 pound pork sausage (Italian)
1 cup Burgundy wine
salt and pepper to taste
basil and oregano to taste

Thinly slice garlic and chop onion and pepper.
Brown the vegetables in oil. Add meat and cook over medium heat until done. Drain excess grease and add red wine to deglaze the pan. Add tomato paste and three cans of water. Add the baking soda and sugar to help remove the acid from the tomatoes. Add the remaining ingredients and let simmer for an hour. Serve over pasta.

Danno's Corned Beef

1 Corned Beef Brisket, about 3-4 pounds

Rinse the brine away from the brisket and throw away the little spice package that comes with it. Put it in a pot and cover by about 1" with cold water. Bring just to a boil, skim, and reduce to a simmer. Add the following:

Parades

Every year in honor of St. Joseph's Day and St. Patrick's Day, there are several parades throughout the metro area. Marching clubs, bands and floats make their way along the route while parade-goers watch and join in the festivities. Catching cabbages, potatoes and carrots during the parade will certainly help set up your evening meal!

3 fresh bay leaves
1 tablespoon black peppercorns
1 tablespoon whole allspice
1 teaspoon whole cloves
1 tablespoon mustard seeds
1 teaspoon cayenne
1 teaspoon crushed red pepper
1 sprig fresh thyme
2 tablespoons worcestershire
1 tablespoon Creole mustard
2 teaspoons Zatarain's liquid crab boil

Simmer partially covered for about 2 1/2 - 3 Hours or until fork tender. Remove to a cutting board to let stand for about 15 minutes. Slice against the grain, that is, slice it along the long side of the rectangular cut of meat. If you want to make cabbage with it, add your cabbage wedges to the pot at about the last 15-20 minutes of cooking.

Aunt Verlyn's Cabbage Casserole

1 large onion, chopped fine
1/2 head garlic, chopped fine
1 pound ground meat
1 small head cabbage, shredded
1/2 cup Italian bread crumbs
4 eggs beaten slightly
salt & pepper to taste
1 stick margarine
4 pats margarine

Brown onion and garlic in one stick of margarine. Add ground meat. Brown. Add cabbage. Cook until cabbage wilts. Add bread crumbs, eggs, salt & pepper. Place in buttered casserole dish. Sprinkle with bread crumbs. Dot with pats of margarine. Bake in 300 degree oven for half an hour.

Irish Coffee

1 cup hot coffee
1 1/2 ounce Irish whisky
1 tablespoon sugar

Mix together all of the ingredients in a mug and top with whipped cream, if desired.

Irish History

Immigrants from Ireland arrived in large numbers to the Crescent City after the potato famine in 1840. Their efforts played a major role in the building of the city and its infrastructure. This group of hardworking laborers was a key contributor to the building of the city's canal system. Many of these poor Irish immigrants perished as a direct result of the dangers of building a canal and of medical conditions such as yellow fever, cholera and malaria. In the hurricane devastated neighborhood of Lakeview, there is a cross memorial on the Pontchartrain neutral ground placed in honor of the Irish immigrants who lost their lives building the canal to Lake Pontchartrain.

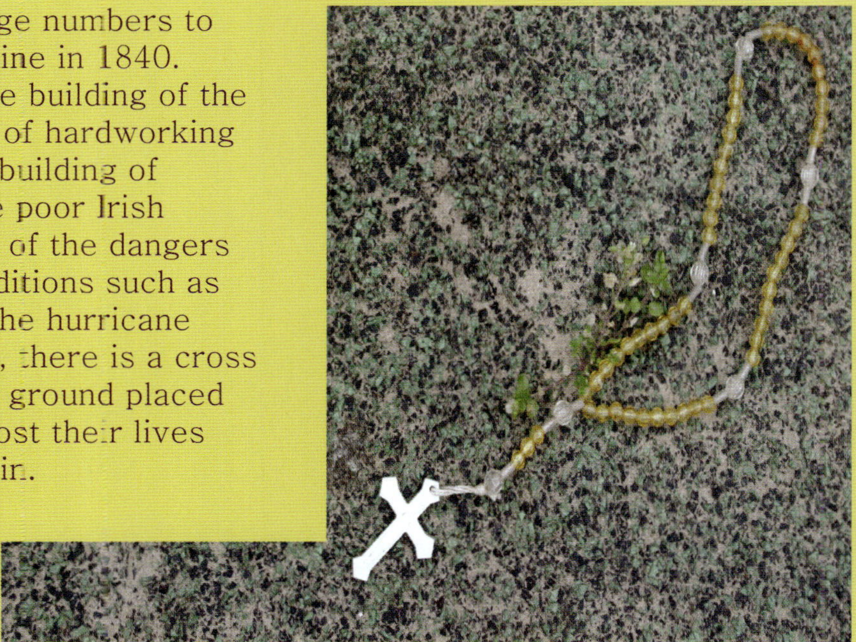

Brocato Inspired Italian Sesame Seed Cookies (Biscotti Regina)

Angelo Brocato
214 N. Carrollton Ave.
New Orleans, LA 70119
504-486-1465
www.angelobroactoicecream.com

2 pounds all purpose flour (about 7 cups)
1 pound shortening
12 ounces sugar
1/2 teaspoon baking powder
2 teaspoons vanilla
1/2-1 cup milk
1 1/2 pounds natural sesame seeds (buy loose at Italian store)

Mix flour, shortening, sugar, baking powder and vanilla. Gradually add milk to moisten the dough. Mix well. Do not add sesame seeds at this time. Let rest for 10 minutes, keep covered. Make a long roll 1 foot long, approximately the diameter of a broomstick. Put seeds across top of board. Roll dough into seeds. Pat top of cookie to make flat. Cut approximately 1 1/2 inches long. May cut on diagonal. Place on ungreased cookie sheet. Bake at 350 degrees, approximately 20 - 30 minutes until brown.

Note: As seen on www.slowfoodusa.com

Memories

Family recipes are cherished, and often handed down from son to son and generation to generation. Angelo Brocato, Sr.'s recipes are no different. Their traditional Italian ice cream, pastries and cookies are prepared from original Sicilian recipes, and generations of patrons have enjoyed them. I'll never forget my Paw Paw's birthday meal before Katrina. I took him, and my mom, to Venezia's on Carrolton for some good Italian food, and then we walked over to Angelo Brocato's for a little dessert. It made me so happy to see the smile on my grandfather's face as he looked into the display case. He was like a kid in a candy store and didn't know where to start. Fig cookies, spumoni cheesecake or cannolies, they all looked good. Since he couldn't decide, we ordered one of each for him and gelato for us. When we left, there wasn't a crumb on his plate. Boy I miss that place! Despite the counter top high water, they have plans to return and hopefully in time for Paw Paw's next birthday.

Brocato Inspired Italian Fig Cookies (Cuccidati)

1 (14 ounce) package dried figs (cut off stems)
1 cup chopped pecans
1/2 pint candied mix fruit
8 ounces raisins
1 pack dates
1 fresh orange, juiced
Grind all together well. Make 1 day or so before. May use orange marmalade, almonds or cherries. Mix well and refrigerate until ready to use.

Dough

1/2 cup sugar
1 stick butter
2 whole eggs, room temperature
1/4 cups all purpose flour (Gold Medal)
1/2 teaspoon baking powder
1/4 cup evaporated cream (Pet milk)
2 tablespoons almond extract (may substitute vanilla)

Cream sugar and butter together in a large mixing bowl with mixer. (Approximately 5-10 minutes until sugar is completely dissolved) In another bowl, add well-beaten eggs, cream and almond extract. Then fold into sugar and butter mixture. Beat approximately 5 minute. In another bowl, mix flour and baking powder. Gradually add flour mixture to sugar, butter, and cream mixture. Add flour until mixture has a putty consistency and mix well. Roll into a large ball. Cover with towel or roll in towel and let rest for 5 minutes. Break pieces off. Roll on board 1 foot long (broom stick diameter). Roll flat. Fill with fig mixture. Pinch dough seams well and roll again. Be sure seam is at bottom when placed in pan. Cut cookies 1 1/2 inches long on slant. Bake in an ungreased cookie sheet for 10 minutes at 350 degrees. Check to make sure cookies are cooked through. Cookies may be iced when cool.

Icing

1 1/2 cup powdered sugar
1/2 cup cream
Mix ingredients well, use food coloring if desired. (always pastels) With a brush or fingers, ice the top side of the cookie. Sprinkle with crystal candy if desired.

Note: As seen on www.slowfoodusa.com

Crawfish Boil & Dough Pies

Boiled Crawfish & Veggies

Potato Salad
Corn & Crawfish Soup
Roasted Garlic Spread

Sweet Dough Pies

Fig
Bouille
Chocolate
Blackberry
Peach
Pineapple
Icing

Restaurant August:
Salad August
Down Home Crawfish Pie

Sweet Dough Pies

Throughout this project, I have met many fascinating people and have acquired many great new recipes. Karen's family tradition of Sweet Dough Pies on Good Friday stands out as "tops" on my list. Until I embarked on this project, I had never spoken with Karen. A genuine Louisiana lady, she greeted my request for family favorites with passion and fervor.

Karen's family tradition of creating sweet dough pies dates back over fifty years to her grandmother. Every Holy Week the women in the family baked pies on Holy Thursday. Karen's grandmother made large half moon shaped pies. Karen noticed that many pies were being wasted because everyone wanted to taste numerous pies and decided to make smaller pies so more people could enjoy the variety. There would also be fewer pieces and parts left over. With so many family members living nearby, the cousins, aunts, moms and sisters all get together and cook as a family. The men would often take the kids crawfishing to ensure the children were out of the way.

Years later, they realized the more the merrier and changed the baking day to Good Friday so more female family members could participate. At the end of the day, the entire family then gathers for a large crawfish boil.

Their family tradition turns out hundreds of pies to share with neighbors and friends for Easter. Every year, the pies are a little bit different. Karen assures me that perfection comes only with years of practice at a mentor's side.

Crawfish Boil

40 pounds crawfish
1 large jar Zatarain's powder crab boil
1 bottle Zatarain's liquid crab boil
smoked sausage
hot dogs
4 packs mushrooms
1 sack red potatoes
24 frozen corn on the cob
6 heads garlic
6-9 lemons
4 limes
celery
onions
5 large sweet potatoes
asparagus
green beans

"Our family likes to have two pots going at one time. The veggies will often absorb too much of the seasoning. You can monitor the flavor of the vegetables by boiling them in their own pot." Amy

Fill ice chest with live crawfish and soak in salty cold water. This will purge the crawfish of excess mud. In a large crawfish pot, bring to a boil the seasonings, 5 squeezed lemons, 2 squeezed limes. When it boils, add crawfish and bring back to a boil. When the pot boils again, turn off the flame, add a bag of ice and cover for 25 minutes. You may also hose off the outside of the pot. If the crawfish are not spicy enough, add more seasoning and let soak longer.

Veggie Boil

In a large crawfish pot, bring to a boil the seasonings, 4 squeezed lemons, 2 squeezed limes, potatoes, garlic, celery, sausage, hotdogs and onions. When it boils, turn off flame an add asparagus, green beans, frozen corn and mushrooms. Cover and let sit 15 minutes. Hose outside of the pot to cool it down. You can also add a bag of ice. If it is not spicy enough, you can soak it longer.

Potato Salad

2 pounds crawfish boil potatoes
leftover garlic to taste
3 boiled eggs, chopped
1 rib celery, chopped
1/2 red onion, chopped
2 green onions, chopped
2 teaspoons Creole mustard
1 1/2 cups mayonnaise

Peel and chop potatoes and add to a large bowl with boiled eggs, celery, onion and green onions. Toss with mustard and mayonnaise and garlic. Chill for 3-4 hours. Serve cold.

Corn and Crawfish Soup

8 ounces crawfish tails
2 tablespoons butter
1 can cream of celery soup
1 can evaporated milk
1 can cream corn
Tony's to taste

Heat butter, celery, soup, milk and cream corn over medium heat until warm. Add crawfish tails and season to taste with Tony's. Serve hot.

Four Seasons

Louisiana has four seasons: crawfish, crab, shrimp and hurricane. The first three are eagerly awaited and hope to be endless. The last, we hope has already ended, never to start again. The good news, we can predict all of the seasons in New Orleans and prepare accordingly. Does anyone know, when earthquake season is in California?

Roasted Garlic Spread

4 heads leftover crawfish boil garlic
1/4 cup olive oil

Place peeled garlic in the food processor. Begin to pulse and slowly add olive oil until a creamy consistency is reached. Serve over hot French bread. This can be frozen in ice cube trays and then placed in a freezer bag. Defrost at room temperature for each use. Spread over french bread and sprinkle with Parmesan cheese. Toast in oven before serving.

"I never thought I'd own waterfront property, with oil!"

The Weather Channel

According to the Weather Channel, if a category three storm were to approach New York City, 3.3 million people would need to evacuate. Wall Street would potentially be ten floors under water. New York City is the third most vulnerable city after New Orleans and Miami when it comes to hurricanes.

Sweet Dough Pies

2 eggs
1 cup sugar
3/4 cup of butter Crisco
4 teaspoons baking powder
1/2 teaspoons baking soda
1/2 cup milk
2 teaspoons vanilla
3 1/2 cups flour

Beat eggs and sugar until well blended with an electric mixer. Add Crisco and mix until creamy. Mix in baking powder and baking soda. Add milk and vanilla and mix well. Add flour one cup at a time until the mixture is the consistency of a pie dough or sugar cookie batter. (Note: You may not need all of the flour, you may need more, and it varies by batch. Less flour is better than too much. You can always add more when you roll out the dough. Too much flour makes the dough crack.) Roll dough out on a floured surface. Roll out into circles about half the size of a pie crust, about 7 inches. Put the filling in the center and fold it in half moon shape and crimp the edges with a fork to seal well. Bake at 400 degrees for 10-15 minutes or until golden brown.

Fig

1 quart fig preserves mashed
1/4 cup flour

Heat in a pot for 10-15 minutes until well blended and thickened.

Bouille

1 cup sugar
6 tablespoons flour
2 cups milk
2 eggs

Mix flour and sugar together, and then gradually add 2 cups milk. Temper in two beaten eggs and cook over low heat until pudding consistency.

Chocolate

1 cup sugar
6 tablespoons flour
2 1/2 cups milk
2 eggs
1/4 cup cocoa powder

Debris

Over 55 million cubic yards of debris have been collected in the New Orleans area. You could fill the Superdome 11 times with that much trash. Imagine all the food in those refrigerators; think about what is in yours! Redfish, ground beef, eggs, milk, ice cream and ketchup! How naive are we? There was a time when a hurricane was a drink that tourists enjoyed, not something they avoided. There was a time when you "axed" only questions, not your attic, and debris was all the good stuff at the bottom of your roast beef pot, not your house. Boy, have things changed!

Mix flour and sugar together, and then gradually add 2 cups milk and cocoa powder. Temper in two beaten eggs. Cook over low heat until pudding consistency. The remaining milk can be added if necessary.

Blackberry

1 bag of frozen blackberries (or 2 cups of fresh blackberries)
1 1/2 cup of sugar
1 cup flour

Bring blackberries, 1/2 cup sugar and water to a boil over low - medium heat. While this is cooking, mix 1 of cup sugar and 1 cup of flour in a bowl and gradually add to blackberry mixture. It will begin to thicken and continue to thicken after cooled. If it is too thick, add a little more water; if it needs to be sweeter, add a little more sugar.

Note: for fresh blackberries add about 1/4 cup water to the berries and soak overnight.

Peach

1 bag frozen peaches
3/4 cup sugar
1 teaspoon cinnamon
1/4 cup water

Cook over low medium heat peaches, sugar, cinnamon and water. To thicken, make slurry of cornstarch and cold water and gradually add while stirring constantly. If you don't stir constantly, the slurry will clump up. Again if you've made it too thick, add little water.

Pineapple

> Left over dough and filling? Try mixing the filling together with the leftover dough and a little flour until it can be rolled into balls. Bake according to the dough pie directions. This makes a great breakfast treat.

1 large can pineapple, drained
3/4 cup sugar

Cook over low –medium heat pineapple, sugar and water
To thicken, make a slurry of cornstarch and cold water and gradually add while stirring constantly to avoid clumping. Again if you've made it too thick, add little water.

Dough Pie Slurry

Place 4 heaping tablespoons cornstarch in a bowl. Slowly add water a teaspoon at a time until the mixture is just wet enough to stir.

Icing

2 1/2 cups powdered sugar ,sifted
1 tablespoon butter, softened
1 tablespoon light corn syrup
4 tablespoons water

Mix, water, sugar, butter and corn syrup until spreadable. You can add more water to make it pourable.

Restaurant August
301 Tchoupitoulas Street
New Orleans, LA 70130
504-299-9777
www.restaurantaugust.com

Salad August

1 bag spring salad mix (assorted lettuce)
9 ounces Point Reyes blue cheese
6 pieces pumpkin seed brittle
6 ounces feinschmecker dressing (see recipe)
1 tablespoon finely cut chives
6 sprigs fresh chervil
6 sprigs fresh dill

Feinschmecker Dressing "August Salad Vinaigrette"

2 quarts rich chicken stock
5 shallots, minced
2 sprigs fresh thyme

Simmer together the stock, shallots and thyme and reduce by half. Strain and reserve for later use.

3/4 quart walnut oil
1/4 quart grape seed oil
1/4 quart extra virgin olive oil
1/4 quart canola salad oil
4 tablespoons pumpkin seed oil
1/4 quart balsamic vinegar
1/4 quart 30 year sherry vinegar
2 tablespoons rice wine vinegar

In a large mixing bowl, combine broth, vinegar and a couple dashes of sugar. While briskly whisking, add the oils in a slow but steady stream. Season to taste with salt, pepper and a touch of sugar if necessary. To serve, simply toss the lettuces with the dressing. Arrange on a plate and top with the blue cheese, brittle and fresh herbs.

Chef John Besh

The immediate aftermath of Hurricane Katrina found Chef John Besh of Restaurant August in a rowboat, looking for staff members in the flooded streets of New Orleans. With his wife and four young sons evacuated safely to North Carolina, he remained focused on his other family, his restaurant team.

Within days, Besh was serving red beans and rice to relief workers. He flew to Washington, DC to participate in "Po-Boy Power!" an event organized by fellow chefs that raised over $27,000 in just one two-hour stretch, one po-boy at a time.

Down Home Crawfish Pie

4 tablespoons extra virgin olive oil
3 tablespoons flour
1 1/2 cups onions, small diced
1/4 cup bell peppers, small diced
1/4 cup celery, minced
1 1/2 teaspoons salt
1/4 teaspoon cayenne pepper
1/2 teaspoon black pepper
3/4 cup tomatoes, peeled, seeded and diced
1 pound peeled crawfish tails
1 bay leaf
1/2 cup milk
2 dashes Worcestershire sauce
1 (9 inch) prepared pie shell

Preheat oven to 375 degrees. Add half of the oil a large skillet over medium-high heat. Add the flour to the oil and stir until it is incorporated and cook for a few minutes. Add the onions, bell peppers, celery, salt, black pepper, bay leaf and cayenne. Cook the vegetable mixture, while stirring, until golden brown. Add the tomatoes and milk to the mixture and cook for 15 minutes, while stirring prior to adding the crawfish. Allow the crawfish to simmer for two minutes before removing from the heat and cooling the mixture. Pour the chilled crawfish mixture into the prepared 9 inch pie shell and bake for 40 minutes or until the pie shell is golden brown. Remove from the oven, slice into either 6-8 wedges and enjoy.

Pie crust

8 cups all purpose flour
1/2 cup extra virgin olive oil
2 tablespoons salt
cold water to bind

To make pumpkin seed brittle, try the recipe for peanut brittle in this book and substitute pumpkin seeds for the peanuts.

In the kitchen mixer, mix the flour, oil, and salt. Slowly add the water until dough is slightly damp and very firm.

Cinco De Mayo Fiesta

Chile Con Queso
Dawn's Fresh Salsa
Guacamole
Mexican Chicken
Taco Pie
Sopapillas
Frozen Strawberry Margarita

Marisol:
Marisol Menudo

Y'at Speak

Dawlin put ya jackit inda locka and stah awhile. Ya didn't pass bah not ta eat. Lemme fix ya sumpin. Uncle Jawn brawta erster po-boy from Victa's house inda parish dressed wit mynez. It's in da Schwagamanns bag inda ice box. Afta we eat, can ya take me to KB's ta git dat erntment annen we kin git sumpin ta fix da terlit an da zink. Anen git soma dem toitles ya like so much at McKenzie's on da way home an eat em while Mawgus is on. Dear Gawd, don't fogita wrench ya plate inna zink.

Darling, put your jacket in the closet and visit for a while. You didn't visit and plan not to eat, huh? Let me fix you something. Uncle John brought an oyster po-boy from Victor's house in St. Bernard, with mayonnaise. It is in the brown paper grocery bag in the refrigerator. After you eat, can you take me to the drugstore to get the ointment, and then we can get something to fix the toilet and sink. And then we can get some of the turtle sweets that you like so much from McKenzie's bakery on your way home. We can eat them while we watch Morgus on TV. Dear God, don't forget to rinse your plate in the sink.

Where y'at	How are you doing?
Where ya stay	Where do you live?
Makin Groceries	Going grocery shopping
Y'all	You all (all of you)
Ya mama'nem	Your mom and the family
Dem	Them
Der	There
Dis, Dat, Dees and Dos	This, that, these, and those
Turlet, Terlit	Toilet
Zink	Sink
Locka	Closet (locker)
Erster	Oyster
Earl	Oil
Toitles	Turtles
Gawd	God
Hawt	Heart, darling, term of endearment
Shuga, shug	Sugar, term of endearment
Dawlin	Darling, friendly greeting
Berl	Boil
Wrench	Rinse
Da parish	St. Bernard
Jawn	John
Antnee	Anthony
Victah	Victor
Gris Gris	A VOODOO Spell, Bad Luck
Lagniappe	A little something extra
Schwegmans Bag	Paper grocery bag
KB's	Drug Store (K & B Drug Store)
Pass By	Stop by and visit

Neutral Ground- New Orleans term for median or grassy area between streets

Foreshadowing?

Somebody put the Gris Gris on us! Did we ask for it? Should we have seen it coming? We do live in a city where the Superdome is built on an Indian burial ground, where voodoo was once a common practice and where haunted homes and buildings inhabit neighborhoods. I can't help but think, should we have seen this coming and this the end of the world? We had the unheard of, a cool front in the summer and snow on Christmas. Then Katrina hit, and we had levee breaks and two earthquakes in Louisiana! And Tornadoes, well some people believe they were the direct result of FEMA trailers. Before the trailer invasion, there were no tornadoes in the city limits. If we get a plague of locusts coming our way, you all may have to carry on without me! But, until then, I am holding out hope that these are just a coincidences and not foreshadowing.

Chile Con Queso

1 (6 ounce) box Velveeta Cheese Spread
1/4 cup whole milk
1 green Anaheim pepper, seeded and diced
1/4 cup white onion, diced
2 teaspoons cilantro, minced
juice of 1 lime
1/4 teaspoon dried oregano
1/4 teaspoon ground black pepper
pinch of salt
pinch of dried thyme
2 medium tomatoes, seeded and diced
1/4 cup ranchero cheese

Combine Velveeta and milk in a saucepan over medium low heat. Stir often as the cheese melts. Be careful not to burn it. When the cheese is melted add the remaining ingredients, but not tomatoes. Continue to cook over medium low heat for 7 minutes, stirring often to prevent burning. Stir in tomatoes and remove from heat. Pour queso into serving dish, top with crumbled ranchero cheese and serve with tortilla chips.

Ailments

In the grocery line, at a dinner party and at work, one can learn about a variety of ailments, infections, asthma and allergies, that we are all experiencing since the storm. One can also learn the associated treatments whether medical or homemade. There are two others ailments people are experiencing that everyone understands and excuses, "Katrina cough" and "Katrina brain." As of now, there seems to be no antidote.

Dawn's Fresh Salsa

1 pound plum tomatoes, about 6, seeded and chopped
1/4 cup chopped red onion
1/4 cup chopped fresh cilantro
1-2 jalapenos, seeded and chopped
1 tablespoons grated lime zest
1/4 teaspoon salt
1/4 teaspoon pepper

In glass bowl, mix all ingredients and let stand 30 minutes to allow flavors to blend.

Guacamole

2 very ripe avocados
1 tablespoon red onion, chopped
1 teaspoon fresh cilantro, chopped
dash cumin
1 clove garlic, minced
1 teaspoon kosher salt
1 tablespoon fresh lime juice
1 jalapeno, seeded and minced

Cut 1 avocado in half, remove pit, and scoop flesh into medium bowl. Using fork, mash lightly with onion, garlic, jalapeno, cilantro, cumin and 1/8 teaspoon salt until just combined. Halve and pit remaining avocado. Using a dinner knife, carefully cut flesh across and up and down in a grid pattern. Gently scoop flesh from skin; transfer to bowl with mashed avocado mixture. Sprinkle lime juice over and mix lightly with fork until combined but still chunky. Use remaining salt to adjust flavor.

Mexican Style Chicken

1 can cream of chicken soup
2 (8 ounce) pack of shredded cheddar cheese or Mexican blend cheese
1 (8 ounce) container sour cream
1 (2 ounce) can diced green chilies
2 cups of cooked chicken, diced
1 envelope of taco seasoning mix
6 large tortillas

Mix soup, 1 bag of cheese, sour cream, chilies, chicken and taco seasoning mix in a bowl. Spread mixture on large tortilla and fold like a burrito. Place all filled tortillas fold side down in a glass-baking dish. Cover with remaining filling and extra bag of cheese. Bake until bubbly and cheese mixture is melted in a 350 degree oven for about 20 minutes.

Taco Pie

1 pound ground meat
1 envelope taco seasoning
1 onion, chopped
1 (9 inch) pie shell
1 (9 ounce) can Zapp's bean dip or any other canned bean dip
1 bag of shredded cheddar cheese
1 small can diced green chilies
1 (15 ounce) can Rotel drained (diced tomatoes with green chilies)

Brown ground meat and onions. Drain grease and add taco seasoning mix according to package directions. Spread one layer of bean dip on the bottom of the pie shell. Then add the meat mixture. Sprinkle with cheese. Add layer of green chilies and a layer of Rotel. Sprinkle with remaining cheese. Bake in oven according to pie shell directions or until the cheese is bubbly and crust is brown.

Role of the New Culture

Throughout history groups have moved into urban areas after tragedy, turmoil and chaos. Many of these groups were seeking new opportunities and a better way of life for their families. This has not changed; after Katrina, people of various backgrounds are moving into the area seeking opportunity. With them come different traditions, cultures and cuisine. These can only further enhance the flavor of the gumbo that is New Orleans. We welcome them in the rebuilding process and look forward to learning their customs and adding them to the mix.

Sopapillas

2 cans biscuits, uncooked
canola oil
confectioner's sugar
sugar
ground cinnamon
honey
butter

Thaw bread dough according to package directions. Heat oil 3 inches deep in Dutch oven or fryer to 375 degrees. Tear off lumps of dough 3/4" in diameter; stretch thin and drop into oil. Cook, turning, about 1 1/2 minutes or until sopapillas are well browned; drain on paper towels. Serve hot or reheat on baking sheet in a 375 degree oven for about 5 minutes. Sprinkle with powdered sugar or cinnamon sugar or serve with honey and butter.

Frozen Strawberry Margarita

1 (8 ounce) box frozen strawberries in sugar sauce, defrosted
4 ounces sweet and sour mix
2 ounces Tequila

Put about 8 ounces of crushable ice cubes in a blender with blades that are capable of crushing ice. Add 8 ounces of frozen strawberries in sugar sauce. Add sweet and sour mix and tequila. Blend until desired consistency is obtained. Pour in large clear glass and garnish with a strawberry.

Cinco de Mayo

The 5th of May commemorates the victory of the Mexicans over the French army at The Battle Of Puebla in 1862. Many Mexican-Americans and residents of the Mexican capital Puebla celebrate it. It is not, as many people think, Mexican Independence Day, which is actually September 16. Every year in uptown New Orleans there is an entire block party dedicated to Cinco de Mayo. And no, this is not just one more reason to party.

Marisol Menudo

2 pounds honeycomb tripe
1 1/2 pounds veal knuckle
6 cups water
3 medium onions, chopped
4 cloves garlic, minced
2 tablespoons salt
1/2 teaspoon coriander seed
1/2 teaspoon oregano powder
3 teaspoons crushed red pepper
2 teaspoons pepper
4 chipotle chiles, soaked and pureed

Cut tripe into 1 inch squares. Put in a pot with the veal knuckle, half the onions, half the garlic and salt. Cover with water Bring to a boil, reduce heat and simmer until tender, about 1 1/2 hours. Remove tripe and meat from broth. When cool, remove veal from bones and reserve. Add all remaining ingredients to the broth and simmer for 30 minutes on low heat. Add tripe and veal to pot and heat through. Check for salt. And add water if necessary. Serve with a squeeze of lime and warm corn tortillas.

Note: This soup is better if cooled down, refrigerated and reheated.

Due to unfortunate circumstances resulting from hurricane Katrina, Marisol Restaurant is no longer in business.

Chef Pete

Shortly after Hurricane Katrina, Chef Pete Vazquez had an opportunity to return to the city and survey the destruction. He quickly realized that his restaurant was ruined, not from floodwaters, but from wind damage, food spoilage and electrical challenges. With insurance woes, a closed business and a talent for cuisine, he assessed his situation and decided to move forward as best he could.

Many cuisines make up the gumbo of New Orleans cooking, but Chef Pete knew that Latin American foods were poorly represented. He noted a variety of Tex-Mex style restaurants, all of which were in Chef Pete's eyes a misrepresentation of true ethnic food. As he watched the progress of the city, he noticed many Latino workers moving into the area to assist with the clean up and rebuilding efforts but no cuisine available that was familiar to them. So he decided to give back to the construction workers and bring them a little piece of their home, while rebuilding ours.

Chef Pete purchased a new grill, loaded it up in his truck and began cooking for workers throughout the city. He made tamales, burritos, menudo and other things that helped make New Orleans feel like home to its new residents. He wanted to understand and respect the diverse new cultures entering the city and make the food experience for them stronger.

Now that he has welcomed the new members of the community, he will move on to expand his knowledge. Chef Pete has been given new prospects. He sees the loss of his restaurant as a chance to cook for others, see the world, and experience new cultures. His role as a chef is to be an educator, create experiences for diners and provide refined authentic cuisine.

The negative impact of hurricane Katrina will provide him with wonderful experiences. In the future, he plans to travel to Vietnam, be immersed in another new culture, and refine his skills and one day share those experiences with diners.

Lakefront Picnic

Janet's Marinated Cheese
Marinated Green Beans
Coleslaw
The Academy's Greek Pasta Salad
Green Pork Tenderloin
Chaplain Bob's World Famous Apple Cake

Cafe Giovanni:
Flash Fried Softshell Crabs with Southern Comfort
and Tasso Cream Sauce
Vodoo Shrimp

Mrs. Pauline

Sweet Mrs. Pauline is still living a nightmare. No matter what, she can't get away from the effects of hurricane Katrina. Her Chalmette home of 40 years, that she and her husband built and where they raised their kids, was destroyed by floodwaters and a nearby oil spill.

Not only did Mrs.. Pauline lose her home, so did two of her children and their families. Mrs. Pauline's daughter lived two doors away, and her oldest son recently built a house a block away from the childhood home.

In fact, Mrs. Pauline's son had only lived in his new home one night. On the Saturday before Katrina, she helped move into them into the "dream house" that the family built together. Every detail of the home was planned with great pride with every member of the family in mind. It distresses Mrs. Pauline greatly that her autistic grandson was only able to stay one night in a room that he loved and where he finally felt comfortable.

On top of losing the family homes, Mrs. Pauline lost something else that was dear to her, a journal given to her by her children. For several years, Mrs. Pauline would take the ferry to visit her mother in a nursing home across the river. The journal was to keep her occupied on the boat ride each day.

So, three or four times a week she would write in that journal, and after two years, Mrs. Pauline had every page filled. She set it aside in her home for safekeeping and planned to give the book filled with all of her favorite recipes to her grandchildren when they were older.

Mrs. Pauline says that each day she tries to be strong, but as time goes on and progress remains slow, each day she weakens and thinks to herself, "This is unreal!"

The Trinity

In the Catholic Culture, the term "Trinity" refers to God: The Father, Son and Holy Spirit. In Louisiana cooking however, "the trinity" refers to onions, celery and bell peppers. Just as the Holy Trinity is the foundation for the religion, "the trinity" is a foundation of many Creole and Cajun dishes.

Janet's Marinated Cheese

1/2 cup olive oil
1/2 cup white wine vinegar
1/4 cup fresh lime juice
1/2 (7.5 ounce) jar roasted sweet red peppers, drained and diced
3 tablespoons fresh parsley, chopped
3 tablespoons green onions, minced
3 tablespoons fresh cilantro, chopped
1 tablespoon sugar
1/2 teaspoon salt
1/2 teaspoon ground black pepper
1 (8 ounce) package cheddar cheese
1 (8 ounce) package cream cheese, cold

No leftovers guaranteed!!!

In a jar with a tight fitting lid, combine the olive oil, wine vinegar, lime juice, peppers, parsley, green onion, cilantro, sugar, salt and pepper. Shake vigorously to blend. Set aside. Cut the block of Cheddar cheese in half lengthwise. Cut crosswise into 1/4 inch slices to form squares. Repeat with cream cheese. Arrange cheese squares alternately in a shallow baking dish with slices standing on edge. You can arrange in a single long row, or 2 parallel rows, depending on the size of your dish. Pour the marinade from the jar over the cheese slices, cover and refrigerate for at least 8 hours, or overnight. To serve, remove slices to a serving platter so they are still arranged in an alternating pattern. Spoon some of the extra marinade over the cheese, and serve with crackers.

Marinated Green Beans

1 1/2 cups white wine vinegar
1/2 cup olive juice
1 1/2 cups water
1 tablespoon whole black peppercorns
1/2 teaspoons crab boil
1 jalapeno, diced
2 teaspoons kosher salt
2 tablespoons whole mustard seed
1 tablespoon Creole seasoning
4 tablespoons olive juice
4 cloves garlic, sliced
1 red bell pepper, sliced into strips
1 yellow pepper, sliced into strips
1 pound fresh green beans, stem ends trimmed

Place all ingredients, except green beans and peppers, in medium saucepan and bring to boil. Reduce heat and simmer 15 minutes. Place green beans and peppers in shallow dish and pour boiling marinade over top. Cover with plastic wrap. Let green beans, peppers and marinade cool, then place all ingredients into a plastic freezer bag and refrigerate several hours or until ready to serve, turning bag occasionally to distribute marinade. When ready to serve, pour beans and marinade into a container.

Coleslaw

"Thank God for Katrina and that pine tree, now I have the skylight I always wanted."

1 cups green cabbage, shredded
2 cups purple cabbage, shredded
2 tablespoons flour
2 tablespoons sugar
1 teaspoon dry mustard
1/2 teaspoon salt
dash cayenne
2 egg yolks, slightly beaten
1/4 cup milk
1/4 cup vinegar
1 1/2 teaspoons butter

To crisp cabbage, place in a bowl of iced water for 30 minutes. In a small saucepan, combine flour, sugar, mustard, salt and cayenne. Add egg yolks and milk. Cook, stirring constantly over low heat until thick. Add vinegar and butter. Cool thoroughly and pour over well-drained cabbage.

The Academy's Greek Pasta Salad

Dressing:

1 tablespoon Cavendar's Greek Seasoning
1 tablespoon dill weed
1 teaspoon celery seed, whole
1 teaspoon ground celery seed
1/4 teaspoon salt
3 large lemons juiced
6-8 shakes of crystal hot sauce
1/3 cup balsamic vinegar
3/4 cup poppy seed dressing, Brianna's Brand

Mix together in a large measuring cup or easy pour bowl.

Pasta Salad:

1 pack fresh herb tortellini cooked
1 pack fresh cheese tortellini cooked
1 pack of multi color spiral pasta cooked
4 green onions chopped
3 celery ribs chopped
1 red pepper chopped
1 yellow pepper chopped
1 1/2 small baked chickens- all meat removed and chopped
1 cup red grapes- optional
1 cup green grapes- optional

Mix pasta salad ingredients together in an extra large bowl and pour in dressing. If refrigerating overnight, save a small portion of the dressing to top the salad before serving.

Green Pork Tenderloin

2 pork tenderloins, trimmed
2 package good seasons zesty Italian dressing mix
6 tablespoons olive oil
4 tablespoons red wine vinegar
4 tablespoons water
5 green onions, finely chopped
marjoram, thyme and Tony's seasonings to taste

Put all ingredients in blender with olive oil. Blend for 1 minute until fully mixed. Marinate meat over night or for several hours. Inject meat with Cajun Injector for additional flavor. Cook slowly on grill for 30-45 minutes until done. Baste often with marinade. Slice thinly and serve on buns with Creole tomatoes, Blue Plate Mayonnaise and lettuce.

Chaplain Bob's World Famous Apple Cake

4 large apples- Red Delicious cut into
1/4 to 1 inch chunks
2 cups all purpose flour
2 cups sugar
1/2 cup oil
2 eggs
1 teaspoon salt
1 teaspoon fresh nutmeg
2 teaspoons cinnamon
2 teaspoons baking powder

Mix all ingredients and stir by hand until all flour and sugar are wet. This requires a very strong arm because the mix is very dry. Pour into a floured and greased 9 x 13 cake pan. Bake in a preheated oven at 350 degrees for 55 minutes. If you sprinkle the top of the cake with water prior to cooking, the top will be crunchier. Never cover the cake, or it will become soggy. Serve with whipped cream.

Nectar Soda

1 ounce Nectar Soda Syrup
5 ounces club soda
1 ounce cream

Mix ingredients together and serve over ice.

Flash Fried Louisiana Softshell Crabs with Southern Comfort and Tasso Cream Sauce

Cafe Giovanni
117 Rue Decatur
New Orleans, LA 70130
504-529-2154
www.cafegiovanni.com

2 cups all purpose flour
2 teaspoons granulated garlic
2 tablespoons lemon pepper
3 tablespoons rosemary and thyme, chopped fine
2 tablespoons Creole seasoning

Egg Wash
4 each eggs
1 cup milk
blend well

Southern Comfort and Tasso Cream Sauce
1 cup onions, small dice
1 cup green peppers, small dice
1 cup celery, small dice
1/2 cup pimentos
3 tablespoons sugar
1 cup honey
1 cup Southern Comfort
4 cups heavy cream
1 lemon, juiced
2 tablespoons hickory seasoning
1 tablespoon granulated garlic
1 bunch green onions, sliced fine

Crabs
Place one softshell in flour, then egg wash, then back in flour. Fry in 350 degree oil till golden brown. Serve hot topped with sauce.

Sauce
Saute onions in medium sauce pot till translucent and slightly caramelized. Add celery and peppers and pimentos. Saute until all are soft. Add sugar, honey, and Southern Comfort. Let reduce. Add heavy cream and let reduce by half. If necessary, tighten sauce with 1 cup of blonde roux. Finish with green onions and check seasonings.

Vodoo Shrimp

6 jumbo Louisiana shrimp
1/2 cup sweet chili sauce
2 tablespoons garlic butter
1/8 cup green onions
1/8 cup white wine
1/4 cup corn
1/4 cup Vidalia onion
1/2 cup tri-color peppers, chopped small
1/2 mango
1/4 cup tasso
1 tablespoon olive oil
1/2 teaspoon blackened seasoning
3 ounces Sobo noodles, cooked till al-dente

Saute shrimp with blackened seasoning and set aside. In separate pan, saute olive oil, Vidalia onions, peppers, corn, and tasso. Add mango last and toss with sobo noodles. In separate pan saute sweet chili sauce, garlic butter, green onions and white wine. Plate sobo noodle mixture, place shrimp on mixture and top with sweet chili mixture.

Green Space

This is a common topic among the rebuilding community members. What exactly is green space? It seems that many of the outsiders involved in our forever ongoing planning process (rather than doing process) think that we need more parks for kids to play and more open areas for trees, and high rise apartment complexes that "maximize" space. At 1,300 acres, New Orleans City Park is one of the largest urban parks in the country. That large plot of greenspace is certainly enough for a city population of 484,674 when New York's Central Park in Manhattan is 843 acres and Manhattan's population is 1,537,195. Aren't yards green spaces? They have trees, grass, shrubs, gym sets and a place for kids to play! They are a place for bar-b-ques and crawfish boils. Backyards and front yards are places for friends, family and neighbors to gather. We need more neighborhoods and more homes. The green spaces will follow in the form of the well-maintained yards of pride filled citizens.

Ladies Tea Party

Pimento Cheese Sandwiches
Blackened Chicken Sandwiches
Mini Strawberry Pies
E-Ema's Pecan Pie Tarts
Strawberry Fig Jam
Pecan Raisin Pineapple Sandwiches
Dainty Oatmeal Lace Cookies
Chocolate Truffles
Tammy's Champagne Punch
Cafe Brulot

Windsor Court Hotel:

Mrs. Joan

While out on a photo shoot one weekend, I happened upon an oasis of hope and happiness among ruin and hopelessness. Mrs. Joan was gardening, in the only garden for miles. Her smile captured my heart and my attention. I had to stop and speak with her.

Mrs. Joan lives in a home built by her father in 1947 only two blocks away from where she was born. Fifteen years ago she had the opportunity to move back into that childhood home, only to see it nearly destroyed during the flooding after hurricane Katrina.

While her husband worked tirelessly to repair the inside, Mrs. Joan went to work on the outside. She planted flowers, plants, and rye grass and put in a birdbath. She did everything possible to make the place look like home again and then welcomed others to enjoy it with her.

It was obvious that the surge of life from her yard inspired her neighbors. Many would drive by to check on their homes for the first time and see the burst of green in Mrs. Joan's yard.

When I asked her why she did it, she commented that she wanted to show people that everything can be pretty again. And it can. Mrs. Joan and her yard are the proof that life brings hope.

That hope is a result of hard work, determination and love of community, and it can bring you through tough times. If you want to live in a better place, make it a better place. Don't wait around, just do it!

If you take a trip outside of New Orleans into St. Bernard Parish, look for Mrs. Joan's beautiful garden and smile at her strength, love of community and resilience. Without people like her, others wouldn't have the encouragement they need to return home.

Pimento Cheese Sandwiches

1 (8 ounce) block of smoked cheddar cheese, shredded
1 (8 ounce) block of cheddar cheese, shredded
1 (8 ounce) block of cream cheese, softened
3/4 cups of mayonnaise
1 (4 ounce) jar diced pimiento, drained
1 tablespoon sugar
1/2 teaspoon Tony Chachere's

Stir together all ingredients in a bowl and refrigerate. Serve in a bowl with French bread slices on the side.

Blackened Chicken Salad Sandwiches

4-5 cups chicken breast, finely chopped
1 tablespoon sugar
5 tablespoons honey
1/4 cup lemon juice
1/4 cup coarse Dijon mustard
White wine vinegar
Cajun seasoning to taste
Sriracha Sauce (hot chili sauce)
1 red bell pepper, chopped
1 yellow bell pepper, chopped
1 bag shredded carrots
1/2 cup red onion, finely diced
1 1/2 cups of mayonnaise (or until desired consistency)

Stir together the sugar, honey, lemon juice, mustard, vinegar and Cajun Seasoning. Refrigerate for 10 minutes. Cajun seasoning will dissolve and mixture will turn red. Stir red mixture into remaining ingredients except chili sauce and mayonnaise. Stir in mayonnaise until desired consistency is reached. This varies depending on if you like a wet or dry chicken salad. Let sit for 10 more minutes in the refrigerator. Taste and add chili sauce if additional spice is needed. In a bowl, place chicken breasts and add sauce mixture until the desired consistency is reached. Spread chicken salad on sandwich bread.

Mini Strawberry Pies

2 full size pie crusts
or 2 packs of mini pie crusts, baked according to package directions
1 container of cool whip
1 can condensed milk
1/4 cup of lemon juice
1 box of frozen sliced strawberries

Combine cool whip, condensed milk, lemon juice and strawberries. Pour the mixture into pre-baked pie shells. Refrigerate until set.

Note: This pie freezes well and bananas are a nice addition.

E-Ema's Pecan Pie Tarts

1 package of mini pie crusts or 1 unbaked pie shell
1 stick butter
3 large eggs
1 cup light Karo syrup
1 cup sugar
1 pinch salt
1 cup pecans (chopped or whole)
1 teaspoon vanilla
1/4 teaspoon lemon juice
Brown butter over heat. Beat eggs well and temper in remaining ingredients except pecans. Mix well and pour into pie shell and sprinkle pecans on top. Bake a 425 degrees for 10 minutes then reduce to 325 degrees for 30-40 minutes.

"The trick to this recipe is to almost burn the butter. And a 9 inch pie shell may be substituted."
Aimee

Strawberry and Fig Jam

4 cups peeled figs
2 cups sugar
1 large box strawberry jello

Mash peeled figs and add them to a pot with sugar and jello. Cook over medium heat for 20-25 minutes. The longer you cook the mixture, the thicker it will be. Water can be added to thin the mixture.

Pecan Raisin Pineapple Sandwiches

1 (8 ounce) package of cream cheese, softened
1 cup chopped pecans
1 cup chopped golden raisins
1 small can crushed pineapple, well drained and squeezed
1 loaf of sandwich bread
mayonnaise

Mix all ingredients and spread on sandwich bread that has first been spread with mayonnaise. Trim off crust and cut into halves or quarters
Note: Use scant cups so the mixture won't be too thick

Dainty Oatmeal Lace Cookies

1 stick butter
1 cup sugar
1 cup quick oatmeal
1 egg
1 tablespoon vanilla
2 teaspoons flour
1 cup finely chopped pecans

Cream butter and sugar. Add egg, vanilla and blend. Add oatmeal, flour and nuts. Mix well. Drop from a demitasse spoon 2 inches apart on foil lined cookie sheet. It is important to give them plenty of room to spread as they cook. Bake at 350 degrees for 8-10 minutes. Cool for two minutes and slide or peel off the foil.

Chocolate Truffles

8 ounces good-quality semisweet chocolate, chopped
1/2 cup heavy cream
2 tablespoons liqueur such as Cognac or Grand Marnier or plain vanilla extract
1/2 cup unsweetened cocoa, sifted

Place chocolate in a bowl. Bring cream to a boil in a small, heavy saucepan. Pour cream over chocolate. Let stand for 3 to 5 minutes; gently stir until smooth. Add liqueur and stir to combine. Cover loosely with plastic wrap and refrigerate until firm, at least 3 hours. Using a spoon, scoop up 1 teaspoon of chocolate, and quickly roll into a ball about 3/4 inch across. Drop into cocoa; roll each truffle in cocoa to coat. Chill until firm. Note: Scharffen Berger chocolate works best.

Tammy's Champagne Punch

1 bottle pink champagne
2 bottles ginger ale
1 can frozen Hawaiian Punch

Pour in punch bowl and let sit. Serve over ice.

Coffee and Chicory

At the end of a meal, New Orleanians love their coffee and chicory. This has been a tradition since the 1700's when the French and Spanish occupied the French Quarter. They had a saying about coffee.

"Creoles liked their coffee as black as the devil, strong as death, sweet as love and as hot as hell."

Buddy Stall

Café Brulot

40 whole cloves
2 sticks whole cinnamon broken into pieces
very thin peel of 1/2 lemon
1 quart hot coffee
very thin peel of 1/2 orange
20 cubes of sugar plus 2 cubes per cup
1 cup brandy

Place spices, peel, sugar and brandy into brulot bowl (or pot.) Fill a metal ladle with brandy. Ignite and lower into the brulot bowl. Ladle the flaming mixture for a few minutes and then pour coffee slowly into the brulot bowl. Ladle into cups and serve.

The Windsor Court Hotel
300 Gravier Street
New Orleans, LA 70130
504-596-4773
www.windsorcourthotel.

Tea Scones

4 1/2 pounds flour
12 ounces sugar
3 tablespoons baking powder
1 tablespoon salt
2 1/4 teaspoons baking soda
1 pound butter (11 ounces) cut into walnut size pieces
4 1/2 cups buttermilk
1 1/2 pounds currants

Sift all dry ingredients three times and put in a bowl of the electric mixer. Add the butter and using a paddle, combine until the butter is completely dispersed into the flour. Add the currants, then buttermilk. Mix until a dough forms. Roll out until the thickness of about 1 inch. Use a cutter to create desired shapes. Brush with cream and sprinkle with sugar. Bake in a preheated oven set at 325 degrees for 15 minutes until lightly golden. This recipe makes enough scones for a large tea party, about 75.

The Windsor Court Teas

According to staff at the Windsor Court, teas come in an assortment of flavors and colors. Black tea, semi-fermented tea or Oolong, green tea, tiranes and scented teas.

Many enjoy black teas with sugar and milk, never cream, to smooth the tannins and enhance the flavor. Others prefer tea with a thin slice of lemon. Oolong, green and scented teas are best enjoyed plain or with sugar to appreciate their full fragrance and flavor. A cup of tea contains about half the caffine of the same amount of coffee. Oolong and grean teas contain even less caffine.

My favorite is passion fruit flavored tea. It is a full leaf Chinese black tea blended with passionfruit. It is a wonderful summertime treat. If you prefer an even lighter tea, try lemon verbena.

Ashley and Dwayne

Have you ever felt like you are in a movie? And everyone in the theater is screaming, "What are you doing? Don't go there? Are you crazy?" And as the character, you find yourself thinking, "Oh man, what else is going to happen?"

Well, that is what Ashley felt like when she was allowed only one day to return to her Metairie apartment after the storm. All she wanted to do was pack up her things and relocate to Houston with her fiancée. Hurricane Katrina and job transfers forced her and Dwayne to leave their comfortable lives in New Orleans to start over in a new city.

They planned their time carefully and knew that the hours would be limited. The engaged couple traveled two hours in the opposite direction just to rent the last available U-haul van in Louisiana. They had arranged for a moving company to help load the truck in New Orleans and unload in Houston. Unfortunately, the movers never arrived.

Luckily for Ashley and Dwayne, the National Guard was at a nearby convenience store. When the uniformed men heard of Ashley's plight, they volunteered to assist with the loading. In just a few hours, the couple had everything they owned in the back of a U-haul on its way to Houston.

Their moving day was also the same day that people began voluntary evacuations in Texas for hurricane Rita. The couple drove west on a completely open road and looked at the backed up lanes of traffic heading east. They couldn't help but wonder, "Should we be doing this?"

Ashley and Dwayne reached the city very late in the evening to find yet another series of unexpected events. There were no movers to help, and the apartment they rented, site unseen, had no elevator. To make matters worse, hurricane Rita would be approaching soon.

The kindness of three hardworking men they met along the way saved the day. For less than the cost of a moving company, these three guys worked alongside Ashley and Dwayne to carry their belongings up three flights of stairs. It was nearly midnight before they were done, and the couple was overwhelmed with appreciation.

The two knew that they were fortunate to have saved so many things from New Orleans, so they gave each worker a special gift. One worker was given the extra microwave, the other a lamp and the last, a toaster. That night, Ashley and Dwayne sat in their new home looking at boxes and prepared a list for Rita's arrival.

The next morning, Ashley purchased the necessary survival supplies, called their families and intended to outlast the impending storm. The couple was relieved that they were again spared by another nasty hurricane.

Next Season

Next hurricane season is moments away, and we are without any reassurance for the safety of our homes, neighborhoods and families. The levees are somewhat fixed, the pumps might be turned on, and we are rolling the dice that another levee failure won't happen again. As we prepare for the next evacuation season, I have a few words of wisdom.

Outsmart the traffic and evacuate early; burn your vacation days rather than gas! Even if you are only going 100 miles, plan as if you are driving 900. Prepare enough gas, food and water to get there. Bring your pets, photo albums, address book, anything that cannot be replaced with insurance money and every member of your family with you. If you can't take it, put it in a Ziploc bag, they seemed to work well the last go around! Don't forget to check on elderly neighbors, friends and anyone else you see along the way.

Photograph every room of your house, your yard and anything in between. They may not look the same when you return. Obtain an email address, cell phone number and list of where your close friends are evacuating. Also, stop by the post office on your way out of town and pick up a change of address form; those were tough to get after the last storm. You'll get a heard start.

Spray paint your email address and cell phone number on the plywood on your windows. This will allow returning neighbors, who didn't follow my advice, to get in touch with you. May I go as far as to suggest that you leave your doors unlocked? That way if there is no damage to your doors and windows, the National Guard won't have to break them down!
The looters don't need flooded TV's anyway.

Lastly, don't watch the news. Instead, read a book; treat your evacuation like a vacation. Chances are, it could be a long time before you have another one.

Sweet Indulgence

White Chocolate Chip Cookies
Carrot Cake
Blueberry Pie
Easy Birthday Doberge Cake
Pontchatoula Strawberry Shortcake
Chocolate, Chocolate, Chocolate Cake
Lemon Icebox Pie
Mississippi Mud Pie

Herbsaint:
Chocolate Malt Creme Brule
Sauteed Catfish with Louisiana Shrimp
and Jalapeno Slaw

White Chocolate Chip Cookies

2 1/4 cups of all-purpose flour
1 teaspoon baking soda
1 teaspoon salt
1 stick butter
1/4 cup applesauce
3/4 cup granulated sugar
3/4 cup brown sugar
1 teaspoon vanilla
2 eggs
1 cup semi sweet chocolate morsels
1 cup white chocolate morsels
1 cup chopped pecans

Preheat oven 375 degrees. Combine flour, salt and baking soda in a bowl and set aside. Beat butter, applesauce, sugar, brown sugar and vanilla until creamy. Add eggs one at a time, beating well after each addition. Beat in flour mixture slowly. Add morsels and nuts and stir. Drop by rounded tablespoons onto ungreased cookie sheets. Bake 9-11 minutes until golden brown. Remove to wire rack to cool completely.

What it takes to live Post-K

Heart, compassion and gallons of anti-bacterial gel come to mind. Also, the movie *Groundhog Day* comes to mind when I think of living in New Orleans now. Every day is the same, every conversation is the same and the progress seems almost at a standstill. You must be prepared to drive through devastation, see homelessness, and listen to stories daily and get up and do it all over again while maintaining a positive outlook on your future. Trust me, it takes a lot to live in a devastated city, and faint of heart will not survive. Patience, understanding, a positive outlook and someone you can unload your troubles on are all necessities. You must be strong, resilient and tolerant. Thankfully, the people of New Orleans are, and if they're not, they're learning.

Carrot Cake

2 cups sugar
1 1/2 cup oil
4 eggs
2 cups cake flour
1 teaspoon baking soda
1/2 teaspoon salt
3 cups grated carrots
1 cup chopped walnuts

Combine sugar, oil and eggs, and cream together. Sift together flour, baking soda and salt, add to mixture. Mix well. Add grated carrots and chopped walnuts. Bake at 350 degrees until edges begin to pull away from the sides. Let cool completely before icing. Refrigerate overnight.

Icing for Carrot Cake
1 (8 ounce) package Philadelphia cream cheese, softened
1/2 stick butter, softened
1 box powdered sugar
1 teaspoon vanilla
small amount of Pet milk (evaporated milk) if needed

Combine all ingredients and beat until smooth.

The Comments

A book about post-Katrina New Orleans would not be complete without a comment about the "Chocolate City." In a time when regionalism, localism and unity are the goal, the finish line appeared pushed back when the Mayor of New Orleans made comments that seemed divisive. Between the "Chocolate City" comments and "overrun with Mexicans" comments, it is understandable why New Orleans is not taken seriously in the political arena. If only we could be perceived as a multi-regional, multi-cultural, bi-partisan, diverse city with a culture worth saving, then maybe we would get the positive attention we deserve.

Blueberry Pie

2 packages pie crusts
1 block cream cheese, softened
4 cups blueberries
1 1/2 cups sugar
1 cup water
4 tablespoons flour
1 container Cool Whip

Bake pie shells according to package directions and cool. Spread softened cream cheese into the bottom of the cooked pie shells. In a pot, cook 1 cup berries with sugar, water and flour until thick. Add the remaining berries and let cool. Spread into pie shell and cover with Cool Whip.

Easy Birthday Doberge Cake

Cake
2 Betty Crocker Yellow Cake Mixes (butter recipe)
Follow cake mix directions and cut into 6-8 layers

Ganache
1 cup semisweet or bittersweet chocolate, cut into small pieces
3/4 cup heavy whipping cream
2 tablespoons unsalted butter
1 tablespoon corn syrup

Filling
1 cup of sugar
1/2 cup flour
3 cups of milk
4 eggs
1 1/2 teaspoon vanilla
3.5 ounces Lindt dark chocolate bar

On medium high heat, combine sugar and flour and gradually stir in milk and chopped chocolate. Heat till thick and bubbly, reduce heat and cook 2 minutes more. Remove from heat. Separate eggs yolks and temper yolks into a cup of filling and return to saucepan and bring to a gentle boil. Stir in butter, and vanilla. Cool in fridge and cover with saran wrap so it doesn't form a skin. Smooth filling between layers of the cake and stack them. You may hold it together with a wooden skewer. Pour ganache over top to cover entire cake with chocolate. Cool before serving. The icing will harden.

Pontchatoula Strawberry Shortcake

1 box yellow cake mix (pudding recipe)
4 cups strawberries
1 cup sugar
1 large container Cool Whip
9 inch trifle dish

Clean and slice strawberries and sprinkle with sugar. Refrigerate overnight. Separate the batter into three 9 inch pans and bake according to package directions. Set aside and cool. Spread a one inch layer of Cool Whip in the bottom of the trifle dish. Then spoon a layer of strawberries. Carefully place one cake layer over the top and continue with the layering process. Top with Cool Whip and extra strawberries.

Fema

FEMA is a four-letter word and SBA should probably be; most people in South Louisiana know what that means! Every experience is different. Sometimes you get a very nice person on the phone that seems to understand your needs, listens, but can't really do anything to help you. Other times you get a very rude person that tells you it is your fault that you flooded, be patient it has only been five or seven months and to call back after you fax them the 50 pages you sent last week, again. My advice to those who face future disasters and the possible FEMA experience- BE PATIENT, KEEP INCREDIBLE RECORDS, BUY A FAX MACHINE AND SCHEDULE AT LEAST THREE HOURS OUT OF YOUR DAY TO DEAL WITH THEM. Their job is to do FEMA stuff and your job is to act like all you have to do is FEMA stuff.

Mississippi Mud Pie

1 cup flour
1 cup pecans, chopped
1/2 cup (1 stick) of margarine, melted
1 cup powdered sugar
1 (8 ounce) package of cream cheese (softened)
2 teaspoons vanilla
1 cup prepared whipped topping
2 (3 ounce) packages instant chocolate pudding
3 cups cold milk

Preheat oven to 350 degrees. In a 9X13 pan blend the first 3 ingredients and bake at 350 degrees for 15 minutes. Cool. In a bowl, blend sugar and cream cheese. Add 1 teaspoon vanilla and whipped topping. Spread over baked crust. Chill. Beat pudding, milk and 1 teaspoon vanilla together in another bowl until smooth. Pour over chilled layers and top with additional whipped topping. Garnish with grated chocolate if desired. Refrigerate. Make a day ahead.

Chocolate, Chocolate and Chocolate Cake

1 chocolate devil's food or other chocolate cake mix
1 large package of chocolate instant pudding mix
4 eggs
1 cup sour cream
1/2 cup milk
1 teaspoon vanilla
1/2 cup oil
2 cups chocolate chips
1 can chocolate icing
1 1/2 cups assorted chocolate shavings

Preheat oven to 350 degrees and spray a bunt cake pan or two regular cake pans with no-stick cooking spray. Sprinkle a little of the dry cake mix into the bottom of cake pan to coat. In a mixing bowl, mix cake mix, pudding mix, eggs, sour cream, milk, vanilla and oil. Stir in 2/3 of the chocolate chips. Pour into greased pan and sprinkle the remaining chocolate chips on the top. Bake for 45 minutes. It will not look completely cooked and will not pass the knife test. This is a very gooey cake. Let cool and remove from pan. Cover with chocolate icing and chocolate shavings. This also works great as a multi-layer chocolate cake in 9 inch cake pans.

Lemon Icebox Pie

3 cups graham cracker crumbs
2/3 cup white sugar
3/4 cup butter, melted
2 (8 ounce) packages cream cheese, softened
1/2 cup white sugar
2 (5 ounce) cans evaporated milk, chilled
2 (5 ounce) cans sweetened condensed milk, chilled
1 cup lemon juice

Preheat oven to 375 degrees. Lightly grease a 9x13 inch baking dish. In a medium bowl, mix together graham cracker crumbs and 2/3 cup sugar. Add melted butter or margarine, stirring until ingredients are thoroughly combined. Pat down the mixture by hand into the dish. Bake in preheated oven for 7 minutes. Cool. In a large mixing bowl, beat softened cream cheese until fluffy. Mix in 1/2 cup sugar. Add chilled evaporated milk, chilled condensed milk, and lemon juice. Beat until smooth. Mixture will be firm. Spread mixture into cooled graham cracker crust. Place in freezer until ready to serve. Let the pie set on counter 10 minutes before serving.

Chocolate Malt Creme Brule

Herbsaint
701 St. Charles Ave
New Orleans, LA 70130
504-524-4114
www.herbsaint.com

1 quart cream
1 vanilla bean
1 cup sugar
1/2 cup milk chocolate
1/2 cup malt
10 egg yolks

Steep cream and vanilla. Add malt and milk chocolate until melted. Whish egg and yolk together and temper into cream mixture. Issue custard into ramekins, bake 300 degrees in water bath until just set about 30 minutes. Remove, cool and refrigerate.

Sautéed Catfish with Louisiana Shrimp and Jalapeno Slaw

4-6 (6 ounce) catfish filets
1 cup all-purpose flour
1 cup white cornmeal
1/4 cup vegetable oil
Salt and Pepper to taste
1 cup boiled shrimp, peeled

Slaw

1 cup mirliton, cut in matchsticks
1 cup kohlrabi, cut in matchsticks
1 cup scallions, julienne
1 cup fresh turnips, julienne
1 cup spinach, chopped

Dressing

2 tablespoons minced jalapeno (seedless)
2 tablespoons red wine vinegar
1 tablespoon lemon juice
1 teaspoon Dijon mustard
1 teaspoon capers, chopped
1 egg yolk
1 cup vegetable oil
Salt to taste
Pepper to taste
Cayenne to taste

To cook catfish filets mix flour and cornmeal together. Season catfish with salt and black pepper (a little cayenne too) and coat with the flour mix. Get the oil hot in a large sauté pan and cook catfish for about 4 minutes on each side over medium to high heat. To make the slaw, chop up the boiled shrimp and mix with the slaw vegetables. For the dressing mix everything together except for the oil. You want to whisk in the oil slowly so that it will emulsify (come together.) Mix the slaw and the dressing and serve along side the catfish.

One Potato, Two Potato, Sweet Potato

Maria's Multiregional Cuisine
Sweet Potato Salad

Sweet Potato Crunch
Sweet Potato Muffins
Sweet Potato Gnocchi with Praline Sauce
Haitian Pain Patate
Sweet Potato Pie
Sweet Potato Ravioli

Dorignac's Grocery:
Potato and Leek Soup

Maria

Maria was the "typical New Orleans resident" who doesn't evacuate for hurricanes. Her neighborhood didn't flood for Betsy. So, why should she evacuate for Katrina?

On Sunday morning, she saw her neighbors, and childhood friends, packing up an RV and planning to leave. Maria could hardly believe her eyes; they never left for storms!

She asked them, "Where ya goin?" and they responded, "EVACUATING! Grab your cats and come with us!"

At that moment, Maria realized if she stayed, she would alone. The "typical New Orleanian" decided to leave; she packed her bags and headed for Dallas and watched the destruction during the following days on the news.

As a chef and business owner, Maria is in a very difficult situation. Her business was destroyed, many of her customers have moved, and she is now forced to be a nomadic chef, using unfamiliar kitchens just to stay afloat. But cooking is what keeps Maria going.

She was born to cook. After pursuing a medical career, Maria decided to go to culinary school at the age of thirty and follow her passion. She believes that food creates powerful friendships, brings joy to others and nurtures the spirit.

According to Maria, "Food makes you feel good! And cooking is in my soul!"

Maria is still grieving the loss of a wonderful city and is hopeful that New Orleans can fully recover. Even though her business was shattered, Maria says that all she needs is a place to rub two sticks together, make a fire, and she can create a meal that will bring smiles to the faces of New Orleanians again.

Sweet Potato Salad

Maria's Multiregional Cuisine
www.mariascuisine.com

4 large sweet potatoes
3 limes juiced
1 bunch cilantro
olive oil to toss
salt to taste
crushed red pepper to taste
cumin pinch or more to taste

Bake sweet potatoes in 400 degree oven until firm-soft but not mushy. let potatoes cool. Peel and cut potatoes into medium dice. Add chopped cilantro and rest of ingredients to your personal taste.

Sweet Potato Crunch

3 cups cooked, peeled and smashed sweet potatoes
1/2 cup sugar
1 stick butter
2 eggs, beaten
1 teaspoons vanilla
1/3 cup milk
1 teaspoon cinnamon
1 teaspoon nutmeg

Topping:
1/3 cup butter
1 cup plain flour
1 cup brown sugar
1 cup chop nuts

Mix all ingredients except for topping. Pour in greased 3-quart casserole. Melt butter and add flour, sugar and nuts. Put on topping. Bake at 350 degrees for 30 minutes.

Sweet Potato Muffins

1/2 cup butter
1 1/4 cups sugar
2 eggs
1 cup milk
1 1/4 cups mashed sweet potatoes
1 1/2 cups flour
2 teaspoons baking powder
1/4 teaspoon salt
1 teaspoon cinnamon
1/4 teaspoon nutmeg
1/4 cup finely chopped pecans

" I wish I had my old problems back"

Cream butter and sugar. Add eggs and mix with sweet potatoes. Sift dry ingredients all alternately with mix. Fold in pecans. Bake in greased muffin tins at 375 degrees for 20-25 minutes.

Gnocchi with Praline Sauce

3 large sweet potatoes, preferably Beauregard
1 (12 ounce) container fresh ricotta cheese, drained
1 cup finely grated Parmesan cheese (about 3 ounces)
4 tablespoons brown sugar
2 teaspoons
1/2 teaspoon freshly ground nutmeg
2 3/4 cups all-purpose flour
1 cup butter

Wash potatoes and lightly brush with olive oil. Wrap in foil and bake in a preheated 350 degree oven for one hour. Cut potatoes in half and scrape sweet potato flesh into medium bowl and mash; transfer 3 cups to large bowl. Add ricotta cheese, Parmesan cheese, brown sugar, 2 teaspoons salt, and nutmeg and blend. Mix in flour, about 1/2 cup at a time, until soft dough forms. Take a handful of dough and roll it out on a flat surface and make a long rope or strand. Make a cut every 1/2 inch to create a round dumpling shape. Bring a pot of water to a soft boil. Drop about 6 gnocchi at a time into the water and cook until soft and floating about 5 minutes. Cool on a baking sheet. When ready to serve drain excess water.

Praline Sauce

2 cups brown sugar
3 tablespoons margarine
1 1/2 tablespoons bourbon
1/2 teaspoons baking soda
1 cup buttermilk

In a very large pot (mixture foams up while cooking), cook sugar, margarine, baking soda, and buttermilk on medium heat, stirring frequently until sugar is dissolved. Mixture will foam, stir well. Add bourbon and cook for 20 minutes then reduce heat and keep warm.

The Beauregard

You can do just about anything to a sweet potato, and it still tastes great. The Beauregard sweet potato is a farmer's market favorite and has certainly won the taste test in our family. It is just sweet enough, looks great and will grow in a home garden. If you have the option, use the Louisiana Beauregard in all of the recipes in this chapter.

Serve gnocchi at room temperature or heated in the microwave for about 40 seconds and cover in praline sauce. We actually served it like a gnocchi fondue. Everyone dipped the gnocchi in the praline sauce at the table.

What can we do with the leftovers?

Whisk together, 2 cups of cream, 12 eggs and 1 teaspoon vanilla. Stir in leftover pain patate. Toss with a loaf of day old French bread, cubed. Place in a baking dish. Pour remaining liquid over the top and bake on 350 degrees for 45 minutes in a water bath. This is an excellent dessert or breakfast dish.

Haitian Pain Patate

4 pounds sweet potatoes (patate)
4 bananas well ripened, peeled and mashed
1/2 cup of Crisco Shortening
1 can Coco Lopez
1 can coconut milk or 8 ounces evaporated milk
4 tablespoons butter
3/4 cup brown sugar
2 1/2 tablespoons vanilla extract
1 tablespoon cinnamon
1 teaspoon fresh nutmeg
1/2 teaspoon salt
1/2 teaspoon black pepper

Preheat oven to 350 degrees. Wash and peel potatoes and grate them. Place in a heavy 8 to 10 quart Dutch oven. Finely grind the coconut milk and bananas using an immersion blender. Then add all remaining ingredients and mix well. Cook on medium heat, stirring constantly with wooden spoon until brown (about 35 to 40 minutes). Simmer for about 5 minutes on low heat. Remove from heat, and mix well. Pour the mixture into a 15 inch oven safe dish. Bake for 35 minutes or until golden brown. Sprinkle with sugar and let sit for 1/2 hour before serving.

Note: raisins are also nice in this dish.

Sweet Potato Pie

1 1/2 cups mashed sweet potatoes
1 stick butter melted
1 1/2 cups sugar
3 tablespoons flour
2 eggs
2/3 cup evaporated milk
1 teaspoon vanilla
9 inch pie shell

Combine all ingredients and pour into a 9 inch unbaked pie shell. Bake at 375 degrees for 45 minutes.

Haitians

French speaking refugees from Saint Domingue, present day Haiti, fled their native home during a revolution. Many began their new lives in the area of New Orleans today known as the By Water. This population played a significant role in the culture and life of Louisiana by bringing with them voodoo and Creole cuisine. Their language has also made an impact today's world, modern day corporations have adopted Haitian words such as pamper, which means diaper.

Sweet Potato Ravioli

1 large sweet potato, baked cooled and mashed
1/3 cup Parmesan cheese, grated
1/3 cup Asiago cheese, grated
1/3 cup Romano cheese, grated
5 tablespoons prosciutto, chopped
1 egg yolk
2 tablespoon fresh parsley, chopped
1/8 teaspoon nutmeg
1/2 teaspoon fresh sage, chopped
Salt and pepper to taste
1 pack wonton wrappers
1/2 stick of butter

Mix potato, cheese, prosciutto, egg, parsley, nutmeg, salt, pepper, and sage together in a bowl. Take a wonton wrapper and brush with butter and place 2 teaspoons of the filling in the center of the wrapper. Cover with another wrapper and press edges together with a fork. Boil a pot of water to a gentle boil. Place wonton into water and boil 5 minutes.

Sauce

1 cup heavy cream
1/2 cup butter
2 cup of Parmesan cheese

Melt butter in a saucepan over medium low heat, add cream and reduce to low and simmer for 5 minutes, add cheese and stir until completely heated.

Dorignac's Grocery
710 Veterans Blvd.
Metairie, LA 70005
504-834-8216
www.dorignacs.com

Potato and Leek Soup

4 cups sliced leeks, white part only
4 cups diced potatoes, or canned potato pearls
5 cups water
3 cups chicken stock
1-1/2 to 2 teaspoons salt or to taste
1/2 cup heavy whipping cream
1/2 cup milk
1/2 cup white wine
1 bay leaf

Slice and rinse leeks. Place water, bay leaf, chicken stock, and leeks in a stock pot. If using fresh potatoes add them now. Boil for 45 minutes then add milk and heavy whipping cream and let simmer. If using canned potatoes, add them now. Add white wine and simmer for about 20 minutes longer. If desired, puree soup. Also can be served hot or cold.

Mr. Jezz

Even after hurricane Katrina, you can still enter the doors of Dorignac's grocery store and buy a container of the best soups around! You can also sit and chat with Mr. Jezz, just like old times! The conversation may be about the food, his old neighborhood, or just the New Orleans he misses everyday. But no matter the conversation, his smiling face is there to offer you support and his good cooking is there to renew your spirt.

Mr. Jezz has been a chef at the store for 11 years. Despite evacuating to Alexandria, losing his home and enduring the long commute from Reserve, Mr. Jezz is cooking up soups, crawfish pies and other goodies to keep the citizens of New Orleans happily fed.

He's known all of his life that being a chef would make him happy. With the guidance of his grandmother and great aunt, Mr. Jezz became incredibly proficient in the kitchen as a child. By his teenage years, he was cooking the family's entire Christmas dinner. He's been cooking in New Orleans for over thirty years and doesn't plan to stop just because of a hurricane.

When I asked Mr. Jezz if he would rebuild his destroyed Gentilly home, his answer was simple.

"Yes indeed! And I can't wait to go back!"

Yes indeed, Mr. Jezz.

Just like the Dorignac's motto, the best is better! Your cooking is some of the best, and New Orleans will be better!

LIL-ARTHUR

The Outdoor Report

Deer Sauce Piquante
Pecan Redfish
Sweet Jalapeno Grilled Quail
Stewed Squirrel
Grilled Roasted Duck Breast
Fried Alligator
Grilled Duck Breast

Gabrielle Restaurant:
Panned Rabbit with Satsuma Sauce

The Marsh

In early November, Keith made his first trip of the season into the marshes of South Louisiana. As a member of the ESPN Redfish Cup, he is no stranger to these swampy waters. He knew in advance that the resources would be limited due to the destruction that took place during Hurricane Katrina.

On his first trip out, he made sure that the truck and boat were filled with gas, that they had all of the food, ice, water and tools that they could possibly need for the two hour drive and day of boating.

Keith was awestruck to see the amount of damage and piles of debris throughout the small fishing towns. Immediately it became clear to him the generations of hardworking fishermen living off the land were nowhere to be found.

As he drove into the boat launch, bulldozers moving trash greeted him, boats wrecked, destroyed and piled up in the street, houses moved far from their piers and very little sign of the old way of life.

There were no commercial fishing boats, no attendants at the launch, and no sign of anything that had been seen on his last visit. When he was finally able to take off into the water, he realized he was playing a risky game of battleship. At any moment, something could sink the boat.

The debris was everywhere, and he was forced to maneuver through graveyards of boats, buildings and piers. On every turn, there was a new obstacle and a constant feeling of apprehension for what was ahead. He had no idea what was underneath the boat and realized that uncertainty could cause trouble.

When he finally arrived to the marsh, or what had been the marsh, he was immediately overwhelmed. Keith felt like he had just lost his own neighborhood, the place where he and his brother have spent numerous good times.

Entire islands were gone, marsh plants were dead and camps that he once visited were completely washed away. Keith knew what the area his GPS (global positioning system) referenced was supposed to look like; only it looked like nothing he had ever seen. He is worried about what future storms can do to this already fragile area. The pipeline canals are full of salt, the trees are dying and this precious natural resource can't take much more punishment.

He worries about the possibilities for his son. He wonders, "Will Ben ever get to enjoy this marshy neighborhood with his big sisters when he gets older? Will he be possibly able to meet the wonderful people who live and work here, and will the area last for generations to come?"

Keith knows in his heart that it will be repaired, and it must be repaired to keep the "Sportsman's Paradise" alive.

Budweiser
BOOYAH
REBEL

Budweiser
CRISP · CLEAN · REFRESHING
YAMAHA
POWER PRO
225

Deer Sauce Piquante

Roux
3 tablespoons bacon drippings or oil
3 tablespoons flour

Make a roux by cooking together the flour and oil until a dark brown.

Microwave Roux

Equal parts of oil and flour should be mixed in a microwave safe bowl. It's best to use a large glass measuring cup with a handle since finished roux is extremely hot. Use 1/2 cup or 2/3 cup of each for a single gumbo or gravy. Mix flour and oil together completely. Microwave uncovered on High for 5 minutes. Stir. microwave 1 minute more. Stir. The color should be light brown. Cook 1 to 1 1/2 minutes more until it reaches a dark brown color. It will be very hot. This roux freezes well.

Sauce Piquant

2-3 pounds of meat
Flour for dredging
1 cup oil
3 onions, chopped
3 cloves of garlic, chopped
1 cup celery, chopped
2 red, yellow and/or orange peppers chopped
2 packs of sliced mushrooms
3 green onions, chopped
1 cup of red wine
2 (8 ounce) cans of tomato sauce
2 cans of Rotel
3 cups of beef broth/stock- more added as needed
1 tablespoon dried thyme
1 tablespoon dried oregano
1 tablespoon dried parsley
2 teaspoons dried basil
4 tablespoons of Worcestershire sauce
3 bay leaves
1 tablespoon sugar
Add to taste:
Salt
Cayenne Pepper
Black Pepper
Garlic Powder
Onion Powder

Dredge meat in flour and sprinkle with cayenne pepper. Pan fry in oil, brown both sides and set aside. Drain oil when finished. In another pot, with fresh oil or bacon drippings, make a roux with oil and flour and cook until dark brown. The roux can take a while. Don't stop stirring and don't let it burn. Add all onions, garlic, peppers, celery and cook down until soft. Add 1/2 cup of red wine to de glaze pan. Add meat, tomato sauce, and Rotel and beef broth. Add thyme, basil, oregano, parsley, mushrooms, green onions, Worcestershire and bay leaves.

Simmer for 3-4 hours covered or until meat is falling apart. Have a glass of wine and wait, then taste! And add onion powder, garlic powder, cayenne, sugar and any left over red wine. You may also need to add more beef stock if too thick. If too thin, remove lid and simmer a little longer. Serve over garlic cheese grits, pasta or rice.

Pecan Redfish

6 redfish filets
2 cups pecan
3 green onions diced, both white and green parts
1 tablespoon garlic, chopped
1 cup bread crumbs
1 cup diced Andouille Sausage
1 stick of butter
2 tablespoons of Crystal Hot Sauce
Worcestershire sauce
Tony Chachere's

Clean filets and sprinkle with Tony's or other Creole Seasoning. Brown diced Andouille in a pan . Add pecans until toasted, add bread crumbs and garlic and sauté a bit more. Remove from pan and place in food processor with green onions. Pulse until well chopped. Lightly brown each filet in a cast iron skillet until browned on each side. Place a heaping handful of stuffing on top of each filet. Bake in the cast iron skillet at 425 degrees for 10 minutes or until completely cooked. Melt a stick of butter in a saucepan and add 2 tablespoons of crystal and two shakes of Worcestershire sauce. Drizzle over redfish and serve with wilted greens.

Sweet Jalapeno Grilled Quail

8-10 cleaned quail, whole or breasts only
1/2 cup of honey
1 lime
1/3 cup of finely diced cilantro
1/2 cup of Diet Coke
1 teaspoon of cayenne pepper
1/2 teaspoon of cumin
1/2 teaspoon of chili powder
2 tablespoons of garlic salt

Mix all ingredients in a mixing bowl, and let the quail soak in the marinade/baste for at least 1 hour. Simply bake or grill the quail until the interior of the quail is 170 degrees. Before serving, baste each quail with a mixture of melted butter and garlic salt. Adjust the amount of garlic salt and butter to meet your taste. Enjoy with a cold Mexican beer and lime.

Louisiana Oil and Gas

Among the 50 states, Louisiana ranks 1st in crude oil production including the outer continental shelf and 2nd in natural gas production.

Stewed Squirrel

8-10 squirrels cut into pieces
4 medium onions chopped
6 cloves of garlic
1 large bell pepper
1 bunch of green onions
2 cups olive oil
3 tablespoons Worcestershire
1 teaspoon cayenne pepper
1 teaspoon black pepper
2 tablespoons salt
1 cup flour

Mix salt and black pepper with flour and pour into a paper grocery bag. Drop squirrel into the bag and shake until the pieces are well floured. Brown squirrel pieces in olive oil in a cast iron pot until golden brown. Add onions, garlic and bell pepper. Cook until tender. Cover with water until it just covers the top of the squirrel. Bring to a boil and lower the fire to simmer. Let simmer for two hours and stir occasionally. Add extra water as needed to make a light gravy. Five minutes before removing from the fire, add green onions, Worcestershire and salt and pepper to taste.

Grilled Roasted Duck Breast

1 cup of salt
8-10 boneless duck breasts
1/3 cup of Tony Chachere's
2 tablespoons of yellow mustard
1 can of Coke
1/3 cup of Worcestershire sauce
1/2 quart of milk
1 bottle of sliced jalapenos or Sweet and Spicy Jalapenos (recipe below)
1 block of mozzarella or cheddar cheese
1 box of toothpicks - soak toothpicks in water for 1 hour before using

Rinse boneless duck breasts and cut them from one end to the other in order to have a fillet, which is about 1/4" thick. Mix salt in about 2 gallons of clean, cold water, stir in to dissolve salt, and add enough ice to make the water VERY COLD. Soak filets in icy salt water for 1 hour. This will remove any blood and "strong taste" from the filets. Next, rinse fillets in clean water and place in a mixing bowl. Add Tony's, mustard, Coke, Worcestershire and milk to the bowl with the fillets. Marinate for at least 4 hours. After 4 or more hours of marinating, stuff each filet with a slice of jalapeno and a piece of Mozzarella cheese. Roll the filet with secure with a toothpick.

Sweet and Spicy Jalapenos

Take one jar of jalapenos and drain all of the juice. Fill the jar up with sugar (approximately 1/2 a cup or until it is packed so tightly, you cannot add more) and add just enough water to dissolve the sugar. Cover and chill overnight.

Grill the duck breast roll until the outside of each roll is medium-well done. The inside of the roll will be a medium color (approx. 165 degrees).

Fried Alligator

5 pounds alligator meat, cut into pieces
1 medium bottle Italian salad dressing
Crystal Hot Sauce
Creole mustard
Tony's to taste
1 cup flour

Season alligator meat with salad dressing, Tony's and Crystal. Let the mixture sit overnight in the refrigerator. Drain off excess dressing and roll in mustard and dredge in flour. Deep fry in oil until golden brown.

Panned Rabbit with Satusuma Sauce

Gabrielle Restaurant
New Location:
438 Henry Clay
New Orleans, LA 70118
www.gabriellerestaurant.com

2 boneless and pounded thin rabbit hind legs
2 cups of seasoned panko bread crumbs
3 beaten eggs
1 cup of olive oil
1 cup of seedless Satsuma juice
1 tablespoon mustard
2 tablespoon unsalted butter
1 tablespoon chopped shallot

Season rabbit legs and dip them in egg mixture. Dredge legs in bread crumbs. Heat oil in skillet. Place each leg in hot skillet and slowly brown each side of the rabbit legs. Cook rabbit till well done and each side is nice and brown. Place each leg on a paper towel and discard any leftover oil in pan.

Sauce

Add shallots to pan and cook till clear. Add Satsuma juice, mustard to cooked shallots and bring to boil. Slowly whip in butter to juice mixture. Place rabbits on plate and pour sauce over them and serve.

Rebuilding

Gabrielle would have celebrated its 14th anniversary if it were not for hurricane Katrina. Greg and Mary, owners of Gabrielle, were amazed by the damage that hurricane Katrina caused to their restaurant on Esplanade Ave. A tree through the kitchen's ventilation system greeted their return to the restaurant. Mold was everywhere, and they had a six-inch high waterline throughout the restaurant. Though they were faced with the challenge of possibly rebuilding, the couple believes that New Orleans will return. Mary believes that New Orleans cannot be washed away, and the lifestyle and culture of New Orleans can't be found anywhere else in the world. She also believes that New Orleanians should look at this event as an opportunity to look towards the future, improve this great city and start over with great expectations. Like many other places in New Orleans, Gabrielle will be rebuilt. The restaurant is moving to a new location, but soon New Orleanians will have the opportunity to sample the fabulous cuisine Gabrielle has to offer.

Music

usic has always been a part of life in New Orleans. In e Crescent City you can enjoy quality music of any pe: Blues, Jazz, Cajun, Zydeco, Gospel, Latin, Brazilian, p-Hop and Caribbean. Despite the floodwaters, area usicians are trying to rebuild their lives, replacing their struments and returning home one by one. Local radio ations and area marching clubs are keeping the music ive post-Katrina.

heck out www.WWOZ.org.

Wash Day

Onion Soup
Creole Tomato Salad
Captain's Red Beans and Rice
Turnip Greens
Cornbread Casserole
Sazerac Cocktail
Praline Cheesecake

Drago's:
Grilled Oysters

The Shelter

When Gerry evacuated New Orleans, he brought only a few things with him. One of those items was his Red Cross vest. For some reason, he thought he might need it in the days ahead. Gerald has a long history of stepping up in times of crisis by volunteering nationwide for the American Red Cross. Because he is a caring citizen, he had every intention of doing the same in his hometown if necessary.

This electrical contractor from just outside of the city limits managed a Red Cross relief shelter in Denham Springs, LA for a short time following Hurricane Katrina. This was one of the only shelters in the area with an infirmary and had constant arrivals of bus loads of evacuees from New Orleans.

During his time at the shelter, Gerry witnessed the mounting stress of the situation on everyone. Many volunteers attempted to follow the concept of, "We won't rest until everyone is helped!" But quickly, they realized the situation was overwhelming, and the need was very great for the 400 people residing there.

People arrived without food, water, shoes or clean clothes. Jerry helped distribute the generosity of neighboring communities. Their attention and contributions were overwhelming, and all of the shelter residents appreciated the support.

The residents of the shelter seemed to be drawn to Gerry because he understood what they were going through. At the time, he didn't know if his home was spared either. But most of all, he understood their accent, and he understood their way of life.

He would often chat with the residents about their neighborhoods, mutual acquaintances and favorite places. Since he was from New Orleans, unlike many of the other volunteers, Gerry was able to identify with the families being forced to leave their neighborhoods and live in a new world of chaos. Throughout this ordeal, he was an evacuee helping other evacuees.

Once Gerry's time was up at the shelter in Denham Springs, he knew that his calling had not yet ended. Gerry cooked and volunteered at a Red Cross kitchen in Jefferson parish and did what he could to help his neighbors in the community.

All this time, Gerry seemed more worried about helping others, than complaining about his personal situation, which he feels is relatively minor when compared to so many others.

Cemeteries

As a child, I wondered how Aunt Mary, her husband and all of their sisters and brothers could fit in one vault. Doesn't that get really crowded? The real story is that after two years, the remains of the family member contained in the tomb are placed in a special bag, moved to the back of the vault and then there is room for the next person. Unlike cemeteries in other parts of the world, the tombs and vaults actually hold remains and are not just for decoration. You may ask yourself why do those New Orleanians go through all of that trouble? Well the answer is simple. New Orleans is below sea level; if you dig two feet, you can reach water. This can certainly pose a problem for burial because there is the risk of coffins actually "popping" out of the ground because of water levels. Thus, we use beautiful and ornate tombs to celebrate the life of those inside.

Refrigerator Wars

Very few New Orleanians are afraid to express themselves, and many saw the clean up efforts after Katrina as their sarcastic destiny. Along with the flooded debris lining the roadside, were numerous refrigerators wrapped in duck tape, sealed for your protection. There were far too many to count. After three to four weeks without power, they were ripe, smelly, ruined and covered in messages. People were speaking to us, through their refrigerators, "Insurance adjuster inside", "Do not open until Christmas", "Free Gumbo" and my favorites, "Are you man enough?" and "Open me, I dare you!"

Onion Soup

1/2 cup olive oil
1/2 cup flour
1 cup sliced leeks, white parts only
2 cups red onions, thinly sliced
3 cups Vidalia onions, thinly sliced
1 1/2 teaspoons salt
1/2 teaspoon cayenne
1/2 teaspoon dry mustard
4 bay leaves
1/2 teaspoon dried leaf thyme
1/2 teaspoon dried leaf oregano
1/2 teaspoon fried leaf basil
2 tablespoons minced garlic
1/2 gallon beef broth
1 cup heavy cream
1/4 stick of butter

In a large sauce pot, cook onions over medium heat until caramelized. Combine the oil and flour together with the onions. Stirring constantly for about 3 to 4 minutes. Add the salt, cayenne, dried mustard, bay leaves, thyme, oregano and basil. Stirring often, cook for about 10 minutes. Add the garlic and continue cooking for 2 minutes. Stir in the broth. Reduce the heat and cook for 1 hour. Before serving, stir in butter and heavy cream. Garnish with hot French bread slices and cheese.

Creole Tomato Salad

3 Creole tomatoes
1 (32 ounce) ball of fresh mozzarella
5 basil leaves, sliced in strips
olive oil
balsamic vinegar

Slice tomatoes into 1/2 inch slices. Slice mozzarella into 1/2 inch slices. Layer on plates and drizzle with olive oil and balsamic vinegar.

Red Beans on Monday

Red Beans and Rice are a Monday night tradition in New Orleans. It dates back to before my great grandmother's time when every Monday was wash day, and every Sunday dinner included ham. Ladies would slowly cook their beans with the ham bone and make a wonderfully rich meal as they washed, dried and ironed the week's laundry. In fact, my great grandmother made such a large pot of beans on Monday, all of her eight grown children would show up with an empty pot to get some for their families. This tradition still continues. My mom makes a big pot of beans and freezes them in plastic containers. When my sister moved into her first apartment, she was given several containers to reheat for dinner. Funny enough, she called my mom the first night and asked for a recipe for rice!

Captain's Red Beans & Rice

2 pounds red kidney beans (soaked overnight)
2 large yellow onions
1 large pepper
1 cup celery, diced
1 pod garlic, minced
1 cup smoked bacon, diced
1/2 cup cooking oil
1 smoked picnic ham
1 bay leaf

Bake ham at 350 degrees for three hours or until meat separates from bone. Keep fat drippings. After ham is baked, fill baking pan with water and boil in oven (covered) for 30 minutes. Let water cool. Separate fat from water. Discard fat. Pour enough water into a heavy pot to cover the beans and add a bay leaf. Remove fat from picnic ham. Carve ham from bone and dice into two-inch squares. Put ham into beans. Bring to a boil, stirring occasionally to keep beans from sticking. Add more water as needed.
In a separate sauté pan pour oil and bacon. Cook over medium heat until bacon is limp, but not fully cooked. Add onions, green pepper, garlic and celery. Cook until vegetables are limp. Add mixture to beans. Stir beans often. Once beans begin to break apart, or begin to stick to pot, reduce heat to medium low. Stir very often, almost constantly. Once desired creaminess is achieved, remove from stove. Add salt and pepper to desired flavor. Refrigerate for five hours. When ready to serve beans, heat on medium temperature until hot, stirring often. Serve over white rice.

If you don't have the time, use Blue Runner canned red beans, New Orleans style instead of dry beans and diced ham. Also, smashing some of the beans helps make the sauce creamy.

Turnip Greens

2 bunches turnip greens and turnips
1/2 pound ham, diced
1/2 cup bacon, diced

Remove stems from turnip greens and wash thoroughly. In a covered saucepan, place greens, water and beat. Cook greens for 30 minutes over medium to low heat. Add turnips, which have been peeled and quartered; continue cooking until greens and turnips are tender, about 30 minutes.

Cornbread Casserole

1 stick butter
1/2 cup water
1 cup (box) Jiffy Corn Bread Mix
2 large eggs
2 cans cream style corn
1 can whole kernel corn drained
1/2 teaspoon onion powder
1/2 teaspoon garlic powder

Melt butter in 9" x 13" baking dish. Beat eggs and water. Add other ingredients and stir well. Pour over melted butter. Spread the butter that will collect in the corners over the top of your casserole. Bake at 350 degrees for 1 hour.

Sazerac Cocktail

1 cube sugar
1 dash Angostura bitters
2 dashes Peychaud bitters
1 1/4 ounces rye whiskey
3 dashes Absinthe or Pernod
twist of lemon

You need two glasses for this dish. Fill one glass with ice and chill. In the other put sugar and enough water to moisten and crush the sugar. You can use a bar spoon or mudler. Add Angostura and Peychaud bitters, whiskey and ice. Stir, mix and chill. Empty the ice from the first glass and dash in the absinthe. Twirl it around to coat the glass and discard the excess. Strain the whiskey mixture into the absinthe glass and twist lemon peel over drink and add. Serve without ice.

Praline Cheesecake

Crust:
1 cup graham cracker crumbs (about 16 squares)
1/4 cup chopped pecans
1/4 cup butter or margarine, melted

Filling:
3 (8 ounce) packages of cream cheese, soften
1 cup brown sugar, firmly packed
3 eggs
1 cup whipping cream
2 teaspoons vanilla

Topping:
1/2 cup brown sugar, firmly packed
1/4 cup butter or margarine

Garnish:
Pecan halves (if desired)

Heat oven to 450 degrees. In a small bowl, combine crust ingredients. Press firmly in bottom of ungreased 9 inch spring form pan. In a large bowl, beat cream cheese at medium speed until smooth and creamy. Gradually beat in 1 cup brown sugar. At low speed, add eggs one at a time, beating just until blended. Add whipping cream and vanilla. Beat until smooth. Pour into crust lined pan. Bake at 450 degrees for 10 minutes. Reduce oven temperature to 250 degrees. Bake an additional 65 to 75 minutes or until center is set. Cool 10 minutes. Carefully remove side of pan. Cool completely. In a small saucepan, combine topping ingredients. Cook over medium heat until thick and well blended, stirring constantly. Spread evenly over top of cooled cheesecake. Garnish with pecan halves. Refrigerate at least 2 hours before serving. Store in refrigerator.

Department of Homeland Security

Many states are vulnerable to hurricanes and floods. Historically, flooding is the nation's single most common natural disaster. Floods can happen just about anywhere. Other hazardous natural events include tornadoes and earthquakes. Tornados are nature's most violent storm, and they can happen anywhere. People at most risk are in "Tornado Alley," as well as areas in Pennsylvania, New York, Connecticut, and Florida. Earthquakes are often thought of as a West Coast issue but 45 states are at moderate to high risk from earthquakes. I guess the point is, no matter where you live bad things can happen. You need to evaluate your risk and be prepared.

Drago's Grilled Oysters

Drago's Restaurant
3232 N. Arnoult
Metairie, LA
www.dragosrestaurant.com

1/2 dozen Louisiana oysters
1 tablespoon butter garlic sauce (see recipe)
Parmesan cheese and Romano cheese

Sauce

10 ounces melted margarine or butter
1 tablespoon black pepper
1 tablespoon white pepper
1 tablespoon granulated garlic
3 tablespoons minced garlic

Combine butter, black pepper, white pepper, granulated garlic and minced garlic.

On outside grill, place half dozen oysters (on the half shell). Put 1 tablespoon butter garlic sauce and sprinkle Parmesan cheese and Romano cheese on each oyster and allow to sauté in shell till oysters curl. Serve hot.
Note: This recipe is as shown by Drago's on www.wdsu.com.

Community

Drago's Restaurant has always been a friend to New Orleanians. Even during the crisis of Hurricane Katrina, Drago's was there for the region. Tommy Citanovich, manager and son of founder Drago Citanovich, lead the way by cooking for members of the community after the storm.

Tommy was inspired by stories of Mrs. Ruth Fertel of Ruth's Chris Steak House giving food to residents after hurricane Betsy. He wanted to offer the same type of assistance to his community and his customers. Despite his personal challenges, he had the energy to help others.

Tommy, his family and several staff members from the restaurant began serving food to the Coast Guard, families and relief workers in the area. The Drago's Restaurant team moved other members of the community to join in the efforts. Numerous companies throughout the area offered food, drinks and other supplies to Tommy and helped offset some of his costs. With the assistance of family, friends, employees and suppliers they served 77,000 free meals to the people of the New Orleans area over six weeks.

As a recipient of one of those meals in the Lakeview area, I can say that they were much appreciated! After weeks of turkey sandwiches and bottled water, it was nice to have a home style meal after a long morning of debris clean up. The generosity of the people at Drago's Restaurant made a difficult situation a little more comfortable for the people of the New Orleans.

Family Dinner

Sensation Salad
Chicken Fricassee
Squash Casserole
Junk and Cheese
Rocky and Carlo's Inspired Green Beans
deBess Bread Pudding
Satsuma Sipper

Jams Poboys:
Joe's Roast Beef

The Cooking Lesson

Daddy gave me my first cooking lesson at the age of nine. The menu was a fine cut of roast that would be stuffed and served with rice and gravy. I was allowed to help him stuff it. He cut little slits in the roast and stuffed them with onions and peppers and then asked me to work on the garlic. So I went to the pantry, grabbed the garlic and began peeling. Then, we stuffed it into the remaining slits in the roast. Our masterpiece was ready for the oven. All we needed to do was wait to enjoy it.

In the meantime, my mother began the rice and gravy. She went to the pantry to get the bag of rice and said, "What happened to my iris bulbs?" You see, many people dig up their bulbs and store them until it is time to replant the next year. My mother stored hers in the pantry.

Unfortunately, Daddy's instruction didn't include properly identifying garlic. I had accidentally peeled my mom's iris bulbs instead of the garlic and stuffed them into the roast. After a good laugh, we all wondered if we could still eat the roast. Since we had put so much time into preparation, it would be a tragedy to not enjoy the meal together.

My mom called the poison control center, and they hung up on her! The operator assumed it was a prank call. Mom immediately called back and said, "This is not a joke; we really need to know, are iris bulbs toxic?" Unfortunately, the answer was yes, they can be toxic, and we were forced to throw out a perfectly prepared, beautifully cooked roast. What a shame! So much for my first kitchen masterpiece!

Tale of Two Cities

New Orleans is truly a tale of two cities: one, a city of excitement, tourism and good times and the other, and a city of devastation, homelessness and distress. It is incredibly important that conventions return, tourists visit and festivals take place. The city needs the revenue and the life. Our lives and our city are in a delicate balance; we attempt to promote the city without forgetting its needs.

Sensation Salad

1 bag romaine lettuce or mixed salad greens
6 tablespoons Romano cheese grated
2 garlic cloves, pressed
Juice of one lemon
1/3 cup olive oil
2/3 cup vegetable oil
salt and pepper to taste

Combine all ingredients in a jar, place lid, shake and serve over salad greens.

Ain't der no More

Locals will understand the Benny Grunch phrase, "ain't der no mo." Before Katrina, we were battling the aint's- Rosenburgs, K & B, Schwegmans, and McKenzie's. The thought of losing more of our beloved local favorites was downright frightening. Our homes "ain't der no more", many of our restaurants "ain't der no more" and many of our favorite things, "ain't der no more." But the one thing I can say is, our spirit, "it sure is der!" We're coming back New Orleans!

1 (6 pound) hen cut up
Tony's to taste
4 tablespoons butter
1/4 cup milk
1/2 cup flour
1 onion, chopped
1 bell pepper, chopped
3 cloves garlic, chopped
1/2 cup green onions, chopped

Season chicken with Tony's. Melt butter in a heavy pot. Dip chicken in milk, dredge in flour and fry in butter until brown. Remove chicken and sauté onion, celery, bell pepper and garlic until tender. Add chicken and enough water to cover. Cook for an hour on low heat until the chicken is tender. Garnish with green onions.

Squash Casserole

10-11 medium squash
1 pound bacon, diced
2 1/2 large onions, finely chopped
1 bag shredded American cheese
1 block pepper cheese, sliced
2 cups Italian bread crumbs

Boil squash until tender and slice 1/4 inch thick. Fry bacon in a skillet with finely chopped onions. Layer a buttered three-quart casserole in the following order: overlapping sliced squash, bacon and onion mixture, cheese and bread crumbs. Repeat layers until all squash is used. Top with a heavy layer of bread crumbs dotted with butter. Bake at 350 degrees for 30 minutes or until cheese is completely melted.

Junk and Cheese

1 pound of pasta cooked (Use an assortment left from the bottom of several bags or boxes.)
4 tablespoons butter
4 tablespoons flour
2 teaspoons mustard powder (dried mustard)
1/4 teaspoons cayenne
1 can cheddar cheese soup
4 tablespoons butter melted
2 teaspoons salt
4 cups milk
1 cup cream
2 cups Cheddar cheese, shredded
2 cups of Colby cheese, shredded

Traffic

If over 300,000 cars flooded during hurricane Katrina, at least 200,000 must have been replaced immediately and are on the road now! New Orleans is now a commuter city and a 60-mile drive in 3 hours is not limited only to the evacuation process. Sit and wait traffic is a part of daily life. Maybe eternal traffic is business as usual in largely populated cities such as New York and Los Angeles, but it exhausting in a city of only 33,000 people. Just wait until all the homes are repaired and the residents really return. Actually, maybe we are already all back, just living in our cars.

Preheat oven to 350 degrees. Combine cheeses together in a bowl. Butter, or spray with nonstick spray, a 13" x 9" baking pan. In a 5 quart pot melt the butter then whisk in flour, mustard, salt, and cayenne. Whisk in milk and cream. Cook, stirring, until thickened and bubbly. Add the soup and almost 3 cups of the shredded cheese. Stir until melted. Add pasta, combine and pour into pan. Sprinkle top with leftover cheese. Bake 20 to 25 minutes, just until heated through and bubbly on the top.

Rocky and Carlo's Inspired Green Beans

Rocky and Carlo's

Romantic, extravagant and upscale are not words that I associate with the place. Rather, an interesting hole in the wall with just the right amount of down home charm and flavor is a more fitting description. I'll never forget my first visit when I was greeted by a sign stating, "Ladies Invited!" And the stories about the cooks and servers are priceless. A friend remembers a visit when a very large cook held his loaf of French bread under her bare arm in 102 degree heat and *axed*, "Ya want gravy on dat dawlin?" It's just something you have to experience once in your life, and I hope the restaurant returns. You gotta see it to believe it, and the green beans and mac and cheese ain't bad either.

2 pounds fresh snap beans cleaned and ends snapped
1 (8 ounce) can of crushed tomatoes
2 garlic cloves pressed
1 onion chopped
1 tablespoons of Tony's
1 1/2 pounds of smoked sausage chopped

Place all ingredients in a crock-pot on high. When it starts to boil, turn it to low until the next day.

deBess Bread Pudding

4 cups of cubed stale French bread
4 eggs
1 cup sugar
1 cup dark brown sugar
1/4 cup molasses
1/4 cup honey
2 teaspoons nutmeg
1 teaspoon fresh grated ginger
2 teaspoons cinnamon
2 tablespoons vanilla extract
1/2 cup unsalted butter softened
1 pint heavy cream
2 cans PET milk

Grease 9 x 13 pan with butter. Place bread cubes in the pan. With an electric mixer beat eggs on high for three minutes until frothy. Add the sugar, brown sugar, molasses, honey, nutmeg, ginger, cinnamon, vanilla, butter, cream and 1 can of PET milk. Mix on low and gradually to high to blend together. Pour the ingredients over the bread into the dish. Add the extra PET milk until the bred can be completely immersed by liquid. Push down to flatten. Let it sit for an hour so that the bread absorbs the mixture. Place the dish in another dish filled part way with water. This creates a water bath. Place in preheated oven at 350 degrees. Once in the oven, lower the heat to 325 degrees for 40-45 minutes. If it is has too much liquid, cook a little longer.

Satsuma Sipper

1 cup fresh squeezed satsuma juice
1 ounce vodka
1 splash grenadine

Shake all ingredients together. Pour over ice and garnish with a cherry.

Jams Poboys
612 Sena Drive
Metairie, LA 70005
504-833-5882

Jams Roast Beef and Gravy by Joe

30-35 pound Round Roast, fat trimmed down to the fat cap and cut in half
2 generous cups crushed garlic
4 tablespoons of steak seasoning
6 tablespoons Tony's Chachere's
5 tablespoons black pepper
1 cup Kitchen Bouquet
2 ounces beef base
5 ounces prepared roux

Place roast in 4 inch deep pan and season with garlic, steak seasoning, Tony's, black pepper and kitchen bouquet. Slap the seasoning into the meat by hand until the meat is completely moistened and seasoned. Place in a preheated oven of 425 degrees and cover with foil for 3 hours until the internal temperature reaches 160 degrees. Remove from oven and cool. For the gravy, strain the juices from the meat pan and heat in a pot over medium high heat. Add beef base and previously prepared roux. Stir until thickened and adjust flavor with Tony's as necessary. Additional Kitchen Bouquet will darken the color. Place sliced roast back into gravy and heat until warm. Serve dressed on Leidenheimer French bread. This makes the best roast beef po-boy around!

The Po-Boy

Benny and Clovis Martin of Raceland, LA are credited with creating the po-boy. They opened a restaurant near the French Market and during the 1920's fed the striking streetcar conductors sandwiches made of French bread for free. They hollered out, "Here comes another po boy!" Thus the po-boy was created. They are served "dressed" with lettuce, tomatoes and mayonnaise.

Opening Day

When Amy, the owner of Jams Po-boys in Metairie, evacuated to Mississippi for hurricane Katrina, she thought it would be a few days of well-needed rest. Like the thousands of other evacuees, she accepted very early that a quick return was not possible. She set out to stay with family in Virginia, and also, like many evacuees, found herself sharing living quarters with nine other people.

Luckily, in mid September, Amy was able to return to her home and begin reopening her business. She worked tirelessly to get the restaurant open two days before the Rita evacuation.

On October 3rd, after hurricane Rita, Jams Poboy's was finally open for business without interruption! That afternoon she found herself facing an overwhelming challenge, a line outside of the restaurant as far as she could see and a ringing phone.

When she answered the call, Amy was finally able to speak with Chef, her head cook from the restaurant that had been out of touch since the storm. Chef called from Texas to say that he was safe. He had been separated from his family, and after weeks of searching, was finally reunited with them. His ordeal included two days on his roof in the Ninth Ward and several days at the New Orleans Convention Center.

Amy was filled with emotions. She was finally able to speak with her dear friend, was troubled by his news and was facing a mob of hungry patrons without him. After she hung up the phone, she took a deep breath and prepared for the arriving crowd.

Despite all of the stress and challenges from the storm, Amy fought to bring her customer's a much-needed smile. She knew that her customers supported the business, and now it was her turn to support them customers. Amy knew that turning away wasn't an option; her customers were thankful that she was there and comforted by her presence.

One after one they ordered; the top choice was a Jams roast beef po-boy! Amy could hardly keep them stocked. She was cooking and carving to order and watching the smiles on their gravy-covered faces. The 60-70 hour weeks were all worth it!

Sunday Brunch

Grilliades
Sweet Bacon for a Crowd
Baked Grits
Mini Cinis
Mimosas
Grandma Maly's Apple Strudel
Prosciutto Cheese Biscuits

Wolfe's of New Orleans
Smoked Mushroom & Parma Prosciutto Frittata
Crawfish and Andouille Sausage

Dan

Dan lived in Uptown New Orleans and, against the urging of others, decided to ride out Hurricane Katrina at home. After the storm had passed, he began to see the floodwaters rise and knew right away there would be problems.

According to Dan, his neighborhood began to look more like Venice than New Orleans, and canoes and boats were traveling through the streets where cars once passed. Many people appeared confused, and most needed assistance to safety.

Dan took note of the many rescue workers in the area moving young couples, the elderly, families and small children out of harm's way. He knew that many of these weary travelers must be very hungry, and he developed a plan to assist in the efforts.

Not only could Dan help save lives and feed families, but he could also help save his neighbors from the foul smells of rotten food their refrigerators upon returning. With the electricity probably off for several day, Dan affectionately looted his neighbors freezers and prepared a bounty.

He fired up their grills, gas burners and more and cooked for everyone. Rescue workers, families and Dan enjoyed a feast.. And when he cooked, it was in true New Orleans style and spirit. He made a fancy spread fit for a king. The rescuers and their guests dined on pancakes for breakfast and chicken and fish coated in toasted nuts with wonderful vinaigrettes in the afternoon. The food he prepared filled their stomachs and renewed their spirits.

His island kitchen even delivered by canoe!

5618

Grillades

8-10 veal cutlets, thinly pounded
2 tablespoons Cajun seasoning blend
1/2 cup flour
1 stick butter
1/2 cup olive oil
1 onion, chopped
3 cloves garlic, minced
1/2 red bell pepper chopped
1/2 yellow bell pepper chopped
1/2 cup celery, finely chopped
2 bay leaves
2 tablespoon Italian seasoning blend
2 cans of Rotel
1 tablespoon Worcestershire sauce
4 cups beef stock
2 tablespoons cornstarch
1/4 cup cool water
2 tablespoons fresh parsley, chopped
salt to taste
black pepper to taste
cooked grits

Grits

Did you know that grits and rice cook after three weeks of sitting in seven feet of floodwaters at New Orleans summertime temperatures? Any proper New Orleanian would avoid buying instant grits or instant rice and would never serve them to a guest, but sometimes I break the rules. After hurricane Katrina, I have another reason why you should never have instant food of any kind in your pantry. I had a pantry full of cooked grits and cooked rice at clean up time. I don't think I can convince myself that standard grits don't cook in that situation, but we will never know. Unfortunately, now everyone is aware that I tarnished my family's name by purchasing instant grits.

Season veal with Cajun seasonings and lightly dredge in flour. Heat butter in a large skillet and sauté the veal until it is lightly browned, about 3 minutes per side. Transfer cooked meat to a baking sheet and keep warm in a 200 degree oven. Heat olive oil in a large saucepan. Sauté the onion, green onion, bell pepper, garlic and celery until tender. Stir in bay leaf and Italian seasoning, and add the Rotel and Worcestershire sauce.
Cook on medium heat for about two hours uncovered. Serve over baked grits.

Sweet Bacon for a Crowd

1 pack of bacon
3 tablespoons brown sugar

Place separated slices on a rack in a shallow pan. Sprinkle with brown sugar. Bake at 400 degrees for ten minutes or until crisp.

Baked Grits

1 cup grits 1/8 teaspoon hot sauce
4 cups boiling water
1 (6 ounce) roll garlic cheese (if unavailable use Velveeta and add garlic powder to taste)
1/2 stick butter
1 cup milk

Cook grits. Add remaining ingredients, Stir until cheese melts. Bake in greased 1 1/2 quart casserole in a 350 degree oven for 30 minutes.

Wine and Champagne

Months after the flood waters entered my home, yet again, I needed a drink! Yes, it is an unfortunate and constant theme throughout this book, and I am seeking help after next hurricane season! Anyway, somehow I rationalized wine that flooded was fine to drink. Don't they retrieve wine from sunken ships in the ocean? What's different about the submerged wine in my house? So, after a three part disinfection process, knowing that alcohol kills germs anyway, I poured myself a glass. I called my mom and mother-in-law, provided my last wishes just in case, and told them I love them. Then I had a sip, and another, and another. I'm fine. So the moral of the story is, flooded wine is safe to drink, quite tasty, as long as you don't overindulge!

Mini Cinis

2 (8 ounce) cans refrigerated crescent rolls
6 tablespoons butter or margarine, softened
1/3 cup firmly packed brown sugar
1/4 cup chopped pecans
1 tablespoon sugar
1 teaspoon ground cinnamon
2/3 cup powdered sugar
1 tablespoon milk or half and half
1/4 teaspoon almond or vanilla extract
1/8 teaspoon salt

Unroll crescent rolls and separate each dough portion along perforation to from 4 rectangles. Press the diagonal perforation to seal.
Stir together the butter and next 4 ingredients. Spread evenly over 1 side of each rectangle. Roll up jelly roll fashion, starting at long end. Gently cut each log into 6 – 1 inch thick slices. Use a serrated knife. Place rolls 1/4 inch apart into 2 8 inch greased cake pans. Bake at 375 degrees for 15 to 18 minutes or until golden. Cool for 5 to 10 minutes. Stir powdered sugar and remaining ingredients together. Drizzle over warm rolls.

Mimosas

2 ounces orange juice
Champagne

Pour orange juice into a champagne glass. Top with chilled champagne, stir very gently, and serve.

Grandma Maly's Apple Strudel

2 1/3 cups flour
1 stick plus 3 tablespoons margarine
2 egg yolks
3 tablespoons water
3 tablespoons vinegar

"My grandmother, Babi's Apple Strudle is awesome. The day of the storm, I made my mom make it for us. Ryan & I ate the entire batch & made her make us more. It is our comfort food!" Nicole

Filling

4-5 apples peeled and shredded finely
1/4 cup melted butter
1/4 cup raisins
1/4 cup graham cracker crumbs
1/4 cup sugar
1 teaspoon cinnamon
1/2 cup chopped pecans

Mix together flour, margarine, 1 yolk, water, and vinegar. Roll out dough mixture and brush with melted butter. Placed on an ungreased cookie sheet. Next, mix together apples, raisins, cookie crumbs, sugar, and cinnamon. Sprinkle dough with apple mixture. Finish edges of the dough so that the filling does not spill out. Any leftover dough can be placed in a cris cross pattern over the filling. Brush with an egg yolk. Bake in a preheated oven at 350 degrees for 30-40 minutes until golden brown.

Prosciutto Cheese Biscuits

2 cups self-rising flour
1 teaspoons Zatarain's Dijon mustard
1/2 cup butter Crisco
1/2 cup shredded cheddar cheese (or use any flavor cheese in your refrigerator)
3/4 cup plus 2 tablespoons milk
4 slices of prosciutto micro waved and crumbled (substitute bacon if necessary)

Combine flour and shortening. Mix in flour 1/2 cup at a time. Add cheese, milk, mustard and prosciutto and stir until it is moist. Turn dough out onto a lightly floured surface and knead lightly 4 or 5 times. Roll dough to 1/2 inch thick and cut with a 2 inch biscuit cutter. Place on an ungreased baking sheet in a 450 degree preheated oven for 10-12 minutes.

Hazmat

Is it really that toxic? Maybe that toxic soup stuff was just the media talking, but it certainly makes you wonder when the entire city looks like a scene from a nuclear war movie. The bombed out look of gray combined with head to toe fashions of construction workers in HAZMAT suits and respirators are everywhere. I even see people on Bourbon Street wearing those SARS masks! Perhaps residents are immune, and only construction workers and vacationing tourists are vulnerable. At least that's what I tell myself everyday. You may look really "hot" in a HAZMAT suit, but in a subtropical climate, they can get a little too hot for me.

Smoked Mushroom and Parma Prosciutto Frittata

Wolfe's in the Warehouse
859 Convention Center Blvd.
New Orleans, LA 70130
504-613-2882
www.wolfesofneworleans.com

1 tablespoon butter
3 whole eggs, whipped
3 tablespoons water
1/4 teaspoon chopped garlic
1 teaspoon Italian parsley, chopped
1/2 cup smoked wild mushrooms
1/8 cup crispy parma prosciutto
2 tablespoons Asiago cheese, grated
salt and black pepper to taste

In a stainless steel mixing bowl, thoroughly whip the eggs, garlic, parsley and water for 2-3 minutes. In a moderate hot non-stick pan melt the butter and add the whipped egg mixture into the omelet pan. Add the smoked mushrooms, parma proscuiutto and Asiago cheese. Turn the fire down to medium low and cook the omelet for two minutes. Remove the pan from the fire and place under a broiler for about a minute without browning the top too much. Place the omelet on a plate and garnish with Hollandaise sauce and micro-greens.

Wolfe's Crawfish and Andouille Sausage

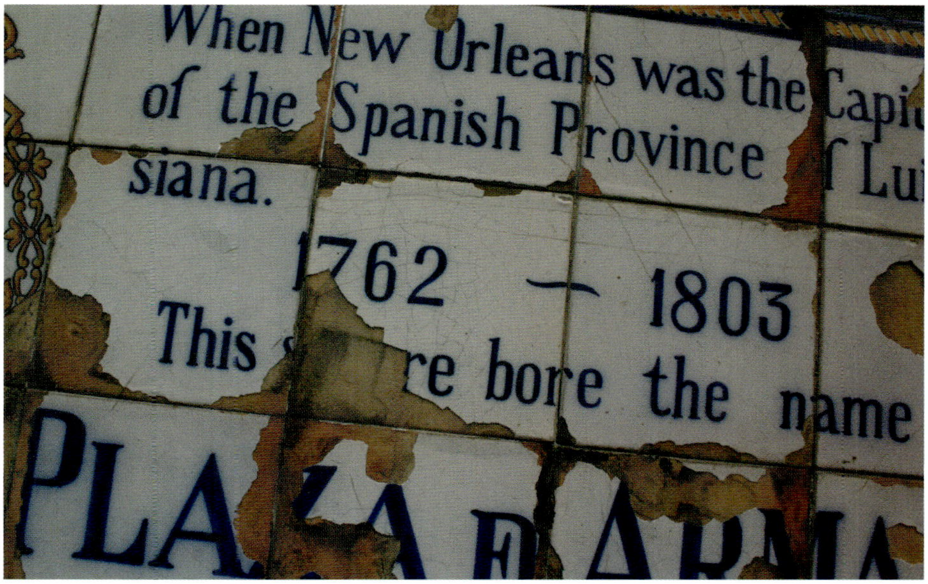

Spice Blend

1 cup garlic powder
1 cup salt-free Creole seasoning blend
1/4 teaspoon chili powder
1/3 cup paprika
1/4 teaspoon crushed red pepper flakes
2 teaspoons ground black pepper
1 1/2 teaspoons salt
1/4 teaspoon cumin
1 teaspoon cayenne pepper
5 tablespoons crawfish juice

Sausage

5 pound pork shoulder diced
1 pound solid pork fat diced and ice cold
8 shallots peeled and minced
3/4 pound Wolfe's Andouille spice blend
2 1/2 pounds Louisiana Crawfish tails

Wolfe's Restaurant
7224 Pontchartrain Boulevard
New Orleans, LA 70124
www.wolfesofneworleans.com
Temporarily closed due to Katrina related damage

Combine pork shoulder, chilled pork fat and shallots in a large mixing bowl. Pass through the meat grinder. Combine spice and crawfish with ground sausage mixture and refrigerate for 24 hours. Remove from refrigerator and form into 32 (3 ounce) patties. Heat outdoor smoker to 300 degrees. Smoke for 35-40 minutes or until thoroughly cooked. It is recommended that the internal temperature reach a minimum of 155 degrees.

Santa Wish List
1. Cat 5 Levees
2. Insurance Checks
3. Fema Trailers
4. Traffic Lights
5. Normal Store Hours
6. Reliable Cell Phones
7. Rebuild New Orleans
8. Coastal Restoration
9. Friends and Family
To Come
Home!
10. One Levee Board

Holiday Gift Party

Gregory's Scarycaine

Pepper Jelly
Granny's Peanut Brittle
Heavenly Hash
Peanut Butter Balls
Kirk's Hot Chocolate Mix
Peanutbutter Fudge
Grandma Cookies
Turtles
Kaluha
Gooch Cookies
Congo Squares

Boulangerie:
Chocolate Muffin

Gregory

After a really long day of dealing with hopeless Katrina related issues, I decided that we needed to celebrate. George and I were fortunate enough to have finally moved into an apartment, and a toast was in order. There was only one problem; I no longer owned any cocktail glasses. They had been offered up to the Katrina clean-up Gods; not to mention, throwing them made me feel much better.

I decided to venture out, into our new neighborhood, to the French Quarter. Surely the liquor stores sold glasses, so I thought. To my unfortunate surprise, there was not a glass to be purchased anywhere around, so I planned to return to the apartment empty handed and ready to toast directly from the bottle. That was when I passed by a hotel bar and saw a smiling gentleman at the door.

Gregory stopped me and asked why I looked so disappointed. Once we started chatting and sharing stories, it was like speaking with an old friend. Gregory and I were in the same boat, please pardon the expression: flooded houses, big messes and family all over the place. He understood my plight, and he understood my reason to celebrate and made me an offering: two sparkling clean martini glasses!

Gregory was born and raised in New Orleans. He and his family members lost 15 houses throughout the New Orleans area as a result of the flooding. He lost everything he owned, including his prized antique watch collection; and, like many other New Orleanians, he was getting the run around from insurance companies.

When he realized that returning home after the storm was not an option, Gregory took shelter with family in New Roads, Louisiana. He assured me that living with over 20 relatives made for a very "cozy" situation.

He was fortunate to have worked for Hillery's in the Hotel St. Marie for four years, and the hotel offered him temporary housing. The aspiring production mogul and entrepreneur was finally able to get some fresh air and a space of his own.

He's been serving up beverages in the Hillery's bar since the storm and has even created one called the Scarycaine. I haven't figured out if he named it after the storm or the fact that it is scary how easy it goes down!

Scarycaine

3 parts orange juice
1 part sour mix
1 part tequila
1 part gin
1 part vodka
1 part rum
1 part triple sec
1/2 part cherry juice

Shake ingredients together in a cocktail shaker. Garnish each glass with a cherry and orange slice. Enjoy, but not too much!

Pepper Jelly

3 large green peppers
1 bottle liquid pectin
3 pods hot pepper, quartered (green or red)
1 1/2 cups cider vinegar
6 1/2 cups sugar
Green or red food coloring

Remove seeds from peppers. Put vinegar and peppers into blender jar. Cover and blend until finely chopped. Pour into saucepan and add sugar. Bring to a rolling boil and boil for 3 minutes, stirring occasionally. Remove from heat and let cool for 2 minutes. Remove foam. Add pectin and food coloring to desired shade of green or red. Stir for 2 minutes. Pour into hot, sterilized glasses and seal.

Mail

What was the saying, "Neither rain nor snow nor heat?" The post office didn't say anything about levee breaks, hurricanes or flooding! Pony Express and carrier pigeons are a much more efficient option for messaging after Katrina. Six months after the storm, you are lucky to receive a magazine, Christmas card or bill. Unfortunately, the bill collectors don't understand that bills really were paid! Insurance companies don't understand either; they insist on mailing settlement checks to flooded out homes. This brings a new meaning to, "The check is in the mail!" Perhaps, it really will be Christmas in July. I'm sure Aunt Emma sent me a present this year; I know she loves me! It must be in the mail too.

Granny's Peanut Brittle

1 1/2 cups white sugar
1/2 cup white corn syrup
1/4 cup water
1 1/2 cups peanuts
2 tablespoons creamy peanut butter
1/2 teaspoon salt
1 1/2 teaspoons baking soda

Spray two cookie sheets with non-stick spray coating. In a 4 quart saucepan over medium-high heat, combine the sugar, corn syrup and water. Heat to boiling and add peanuts. Cook until peanuts become golden in color and syrup mixture beads off nuts when raised out of pan. Quickly mix in the salt and baking soda and peanut butter until well blended. Pour the mixture onto the prepared cookie sheets. Allow mixture to spread on its own. Cool completely, and break into pieces. Store in airtight container. Humidity will ruin the peanut brittle.

Heavenly Hash

2 cups package semi-sweet chocolate chips
1 (14 ounce) can sweetened condensed milk
2 tablespoons butter
2 cups whole toasted walnuts, peanuts or almonds
1 (10 1/2 ounce) bag miniature marshmallows

Melt chocolates, milk and butter in a double boiler; cook and stir until creamy. Remove from heat and stir in nuts and marshmallows. Pour mixture into a bunt cake pan. This makes a beautiful heavenly hash ring. Store in refrigerator.

Peanut Butter Balls

1/2 cup butter, melted
1 1/2 cup creamy peanut butter
2 cups powdered sugar
1 teaspoon vanilla extract
2 cups of chocolate chips
3 tablespoons butter

Combine butter, peanut butter, sugar and vanilla in a large bowl; mix until smooth. Shape mixture into small 1 inch balls. Place on baking sheet. Freeze for one hour. Melt chocolate and butter in a double boiler. Stir constantly until well blended. Place a skewer in the center of a frozen peanut butter ball and cover as much as possible with chocolate. When cooled, take a small portion of chocolate on a fork and shake over tops. This should cover the hole from the skewer and make a pattern on the ball. Return to baking sheet and freeze until ready to serve. Keep refrigerated.

Booze!

The role of alcohol in a post-Katrina world cannot be ignored. It seems like everyone I know is a drinker. I've heard numerous stories about holiday parties that went over budget because the guests' tolerance was too high from the storm related drinking. I knew it was affecting me when one day I found myself in the grocery store with a cart filled with a loaf of bread, two bottles of wine and a bottle of vodka. I was almost embarrassed until I, soberly, collided with another basket filled with a case of wine, a bottle of gin, a bottle of bourbon and a candy bar. At that point I realized, I could be worse. Right? Katrina has probably created her share of alcohol abusers, and most are not in hiding! They are right there in the middle of the grocery line buying booze and not food. Someone call AA!

Kirk's Hot Chocolate Mix

1 (2 pound) box chocolate powder
1 pound powdered sugar
1 (11 ounce) jar Coffeemate
1 (8 ounce) box of powdered milk

Mix together and sift. Store in airtight container. Fill 1/2 cup of mixture and fill remaining cup with hot water.

Peanut Butter Fudge

2 cups sugar
1/2 cup evaporated milk
2 teaspoons margarine
1 teaspoon vanilla
1 small jar peanut butter

Microwave sugar, evaporated milk, and margarine on high for 2 1/2 minutes and stir. Then microwave for another 2 1/2 minutes. Add vanilla and peanut butter and stir. If necessary, microwave for another minute or two. Pour warm mixture into a greased pan, cool and cut into squares.

The Go-Cup

Holidays mean party time, and parties have go cups. It is hard for people from outside of New Orleans to understand the concept of the "go cup." It is exactly as it sounds, a cup you take on the go. One thing that separates this cultural icon from standard "take out" is that a "go cup" contains some sort of alcohol. If you enter a bar and don't finish your beer, pour it into a "go cup" and take it with you. If you go to a party and want a punch for the walk home, put it in a go cup. It is unacceptable to drink an alcoholic beverage on the go from a glass bottle, but perfectly acceptable to drink it from a plastic cup. And it is never acceptable to drink and drive.

Grandma Cookies

1/2 cup plus 2 teaspoons butter
1/2 cup brown sugar, packed
1/2 cup white sugar
1 egg
1/2 teaspoon vanilla
1 cup flour
1/4 teaspoon salt
1/2 teaspoon baking soda
1/4 teaspoon baking powder
1 cup rolled oats
1/2 cup raisins, pecans or candied fruit
1 cup rice krisp cereal

Cream together the butter, brown sugar and white sugar. Add in one egg and vanilla and beat well. Sift together flour, salt, baking soda and baking powder and add to the creamed mixture. Stir in oats, raisins and cereal. Drop by the spoonful on a greased cookie sheet and make in a 350 degree oven for 15 minutes.

Turtles

2 cups pecans, coarsely chopped
1 stick margarine
1 (14 ounce) bag caramels
2 cups milk chocolate chips

Melt margarine and caramels over a double boiler. When melted, slowly add chopped pecans. Using two spoons, scoop and place the mixture on a greased cookie sheet. Let the turtles cool. Clean out the double boiler and then melt the chocolate chips in the double boiler. Dip the turtles in the melted chocolate and place on wax paper.

Kaluha

1 (2 ounce) jar instant coffee
2 cup boiling water
1 bottle vodka
3 cups sugar
1 tablespoon vanilla

Mix all together, put in gallon jug and let stand two weeks. Or pour into individual bottles for holiday gifts.

Gooch Cookies

2 sticks butter
2 cups sugar
1/2 teaspoon baking powder
3 1/2 cups unsifted flour
1/2 teaspoon salt
2 whole eggs
1 egg yolk
2 teaspoons vanilla
1 tablespoon lemon zest, grated

Cream together butter and sugar. Add eggs and egg yolk. Slowly add in flour, baking powder, and salt. Add in vanilla. If the mixture is too stiff, add 2 tablespoons milk. Line a cookie sheet with foil. Cookies can be rolled or pushed through a cookie press and placed on the sheet. Bake in the oven at 325 degrees for 12 minutes. Remove from the oven and cool completely before removing them from the pan.

Congo Squares

2 1/2 cups flour, measured before sifting
1 1/2 teaspoons baking powder
1/2 teaspoon salt
2/3 cup butter
2 1/2 cups brown sugar
3 eggs
2 teaspoons fresh squeezed lemon juice
1 cup pecans
1 (6 ounce) package of chocolate chips

Sift dry ingredients. Melt butter in a large saucepan and remove from the heat and cool slightly. In a bowl, add butter, sugar, eggs and lemon juice. Add dry ingredients while slowly mixing in the dry ingredients. Blend in pecans and chocolate chips. Spread into a 12x8x2 pan. Bake for 25 minutes at 350 degrees.

La Boulangerie
4526 Magazine Street
New Orleans, LA 70115
504-269-3777

Chocolate Muffin

1 pound high quality bittersweet chocolate, finely chopped
3 ounces high quality unsweetened chocolate, finely chopped
1/2 cup plus 2 tablespoons strong brewed coffee
6 large eggs, at room temperature
3/4 cup sugar
1 cup heavy cream

Preheat the oven to 325 degrees. Lightly butter the inside of a 10 inch round cake pan. Line the bottom of the pan with a circle of parchment paper. In the top of a double boiler over simmering water, not boiling, melt the bittersweet and unsweetened chocolates with the coffee.

With an electric mixer, whisk eggs and sugar together in a metal bowl. Set the bowl over a medium pan of simmering water. Whisk until the mixture is warm to the touch and the sugar is desolved, about two minutes. Attach the bowl to the mixer and beat at medium-high speed until light and almost trippled in volume. This should take about three minutes. Reduce the speed to medium-low and continue beating for another two mintues. Set aside. In a chilled bowl, beat the cream just past the soft-peak stage, until it dollops nicely and holds its shape when dropped from a spoon onto a plate. If the cream is too soft, the cake will be airy. If the cream is too firm, it may be dry. Fold a quarter of the egg mixture into the chocolate mixture. Fold this lightened chocolate mixture back into the remaining egg mixture. Fold in the whipped cream. Transfer to the prepared pan, smooth the top and tap the filled pan lightly on the work surface to settle any air pockets. Place the pan in a larger baking pan and put into the oven. Add enough hot water into the baking pan to come halfway up the side of the cake pan. Bake for 30 minutes. Open the oven door for 30 seconds and release any excess moisture that builds in the oven. Continue baking until the center of the cake feels firm, another 20-30 mintues. Let the muffins cool in the turned off oven for two hours.

Communication

The written word and talk radio were the main sources to effectively communicate after Katrina. Text messages were the only way to contact locals and many people resorted to purchasing out of town cell phones to complete a call. The phone lines were jammed and nothing was working but everyone needed to communicate. After the storm, people were writing on everything to speak to friends, family and customers: refrigerators, old sheet rock, the fronts of houses and on millions of little signs lined up in the neutral ground. Miles of messages lined the streets, "we're ok, in Houston", "we found your cat, it's safe", "Cheap roof repairs, call or text my cell" and "100 signs for $99, see our website."

Buffet Holiday Dinner

Karen's Kitchen:

Okra Gumbo

Cajun Fried Turkey

Auntie Nika's Cafeteria Style Rolls

Oyster Dressing Alzina

Patsy's Cornbread Dressing

Granny Gahn's Stuffed Mirliton

Green Bean and Artichoke Casserole

Red Hot Punch

Tiramisu

Arnaud's:

Turtle Soup

Karen and her family

After traveling through the lower Ninth Ward one day, I was overwhelmed by the sights and destruction. While there, I met a family that was standing over the ruins of what was once a home. They were obviously upset and looked as if they were discussing what to do next.

Karen's family, like many others in the New Orleans area, was forced to deal with the loss of several family homes. Her in-laws' Ninth Ward home was completely demolished, while Karen and her husband lost their home in New Orleans East. On top of all that loss, Karen's business was completely destroyed by the flooding in her area. As a caterer, her recipes were her business and most were lost.

With the help of her sister in St. Martinville and her strong faith, Karen and her family are starting over and attempting to get their lives back on track.

When I asked Karen if she was returning to New Orleans, her answer was simple, "YES, YES, YES!"

Karen has teamed up with her sister Rita, and together they have searched their hearts for recipes they loved. With Rita's support, the entire family is recovering, and Karen is returning to a profession she enjoys. Karen and Rita's recipe for okra gumbo won first place in the African American Museum Okra Cookoff in St. Martinville, LA. Enjoy it with your family and know that it is food from the heart and food for the soul.

Okra Gumbo

Karen's Kitchen
Temporary Location
Kade, LA
337-364-5582

2 cups of roux
8 cups of water
1 large onion, chopped
1 large bell pepper, chopped
1 quart cook okra, chopped
3 pounds smoked sausage
1 whole cut up fryer
Seasoning of preference

Place water to boil in large stock pot. Add roux, okra and chopped vegetables to boiling water. Allow roux and vegetables to boil approx. 2 hours. Add sausageand chicken (brown chicken if desire) to water. Season to taste. Let simmer for 1 hour. Serve over steamed rice and enjoy.

Cajun Fried Turkey

12 pound turkey (cleaned)
3 tablespoons garlic
3 sticks butter
3 tablespoons onion juice
1 cup beer, bourbon or other flavorful alcohol
3 1/2 gallons cooking oil
4 tablespoons Crystal hot sauce
1/2 cup Tony's

The Meal

Holiday dinners are very important to families in Louisiana since they are a wonderful time to gather together over a great meal. Each family usually has its own traditions for Christmas and Thanksgiving, and the turkey is not always the focus of the meal. Every holiday, we look forward to the side dishes. It is a learned art to fit a taste of each dish on your plate in one trip. But our favorite part of the day is seconds! Usually about four or five hours after everyone has indulged in too much food, we start to snack. Before you know it, all the dishes are out again and everyone is ready for round two. The day ends with full bellies, warm smiles and good intentions for not overindulging the next year.

Melt butter and add garlic, onion juice, crystal and alcohol. With a large injector (large kitchen syringe) fill with marinade mixture. Inject the mixture into the legs, thighs, wings, back and breast. Rub the outside of the turkey with Tony's. In a 48 quart pot, place oil and heat until oil can light a match. Lower turkey into the oil and cook for 3 minutes per pound. Remove, drain and serve.

Auntie Nika's Cafeteria Style Rolls

2 cups warm water (not quite hot)
2 packages dry yeast
7 tablespoons sugar, divided
1 tablespoons salt
1/4 cup Butter Flavored Crisco shortening
5 1/4 cups all-purpose flour
1/4 cup oil for roll tops

Combine water and 2 tablespoons sugar, stir twice, add yeast and sit until the yeast floats. Add salt, Crisco and remaining 5 tablespoons sugar. Add flour, mix well and stir well. Place in a greased bowl, oil top lightly and allow to rise until doubled in size. Roll out on a floured surface. Shape into rolls and place in greased pan. Brush the top with oil and bake at 400 degrees until browned. Serve warm.

Oyster Dressing Alzina

2 tablespoons butter
1 lb ground chicken gizzards
1 large yellow onion, chopped
2 ribs celery, chopped
1 large bell pepper, chopped
2 cloves garlic, chopped
1 quart oysters in their liquid, chopped
4 cups beef or chicken stock
1 teaspoon Kitchen Bouquet
1/2 cup parsley and green onions, chopped
1/4 teaspoon sugar
salt and pepper to taste
4 cups cooked rice

Sauté first 6 ingredients. Stir in oysters and liquid and remainder of ingredients except rice. Cook for 1 hour on low/medium heat adding stock as needed. Stir in desired amount of rice. Serve hot in a casserole dish. Dressing should not be too wet or dry.

Patsy's Cornbread Dressing

5 cups of Martha White's self-rising cormeal(cornbread)in a bag
2 yellow onions
1 large bell pepper
5 stalks of celery, chopped
2 chicken broth cans
1 stick of real butter
2 teaspoons salt and pepper
1/2 teaspoon poultry seasoning
1/4 teaspoon red pepper

"Voila! The best cornbread dressing Pineville, Lousiana has to offer!!!!"

First cook the Martha White's cornmeal as instructed on bag. Cook the onions, bell pepper, celery, and butter in a pan for 40 minutes on low
Add cooked cornbread to pan with onion, bell pepper, celery and butter
Then add salt, pepper, poultry seasoning, red pepper. Add water if it is dry. Bake 45 mintues a 350 degrees for an hour. Bacon and Sausage are a nice addition to this dressing.

Granny Gahn's Shrimp-Stuffed Mirliton

6 fresh mirlitons
1/4 pound butter
1 cup onions diced
1 cup celery diced
1/4 cup garlic minced
1/4 cup parsley chopped
1 tablespoons fresh basil
12 pats butter
salt and pepper to taste
1 pound fresh shrimp peeled and cut in half
2 cups bread crumbs
bread crumbs to top

Preheat oven to 375 degrees. Boil mirlitons in lightly salted water until pulp is tender enough to scoop from the shells, but leave shells intact, approximately. 30-40 minutes. Once tender, remove from water and cool. Cut in half lengthwise. Using a teaspoon, remove the seedpod from center of mirliton and discard. Gently scoop all pulp out of shell and set aside. Reserve pulp (meat) and save shells for stuffing. In a 12-inch cast iron skillet, melt butter over medium high heat. Add onions, celery, bell peppers, garlic and basil. Sauté 3-5 minutes or until wilted. Add mirliton pulp. Sauté an additional 3-5 minutes. Add shrimp and blend well into the veggie mixture. Cook 15-20 minutes, stirring until flavors develop. After most of the liquid has evaporated, remove from heat and season to taste with salt, pepper and parsley. Sprinkle approximately 1 1/2 cup bread crumbs to absorb an excess liquid. Gently fill shells. Place stuffed mirlitons halves into large casserole dish and sprinkle with bread crumbs. Top each mirliton with 1 pat butter and bake until golden brown, approximately. 30 minutes.

Green Bean and Artichoke Casserole

1/2 cup olive oil
3 cans of Italian flat green beans, liquid drained
l large onion chopped fine
l can of artichoke hearts drained and chopped, liquid drained
1 cup Parmesan cheese
Italian bread crumbs

Fry the onion in olive oil until clear, add the drained beans and artichoke hearts, cook over medium heat until blended. Add Parmesan cheese to taste and add salt and pepper. Remember cheese is salty. Pour into casserole dish, sprinkle with bread crumbs and bake at 350 degrees until bubbly.

Red Hot Punch

1 pound Red Hots Brach's Candy
3 cups strong tea
1 quart pineapple juice
1 quart orange juice
3 sticks whole cloves
1 teaspoon lemon extract
2 quarts water
suagar to taste

Make tea in a large pot. Melt red hots over low heat in the tea. Add all other ingredients and sugar to taste if necessary. Usually the red-hot candy will make it sweet enough, but more sugar can be added. Serve hot and keep in a crockpot or hot pot. This may be reheated on another day after refrigerating.

Naturally Nawlins?

Tiramisu is not a usual New Orleans dessert for Christmas, but it is in my husband's family. Uncle Kurt decided one Christmas he would make a very fancy dish called tiramisu and spent hours assembling it and making it just perfect. When Aunt Lisa went to the back refrigerator to get the turtle soup for Christmas dinner, she made a huge mistake! She pulled the soup out a little too quickly and not only spilled the soup, but also dropped the tiramisu. She immediately started to panic and began trying to "straighten out" the tiramisu. In the process, she spilled more soup. She was so worried that Uncle Kurt would be upset because all of his hard work might go unnoticed. With a little help from her nephew, she did everything possible to make it look like nothing happened. Aunt Lisa put the dish back into the refrigerator thinking no one would be the wiser. Unfortunately, she hadn't anticipated answering the question, "Lisa, why are you all covered in soup and tiramisu?" We have enjoyed Uncle Kurt's tiramisu every year since.

Tiramisu

3 eggs, separated
2 cups mascarpone cheese, at room temperature
1/4 cup vanilla sugar
3/4 cup cold, very strong, black coffee
1/2 cup Kaluha or other coffee flavored liqueur
18 savoiardi (Italian sponge lady fingers)
Sifted cocoa powder

Mix the coffee and liqueur. Whisk the egg whites with an electric mixer until stiff peaks form. Whisk the mascarpone cheese, vanilla sugar, and egg yolks in a separate bowl until evenly combined. Fold in the egg whites. Dip a savoiardi in the coffee & liqueur mixture, turn it quickly so that it becomes saturated but doesn't disintegrate, place it in the bottom of a flat-bottomed serving dish. Make a layer of these across the bottom of the dish. Then spoon in about a third of the mascarpone mixture across the top of this layer and spread it out evenly. Make more layers in the same way, ending with mascarpone. Level the surface, and then sift cocoa powder all over. Cover and chill overnight.

Arnaud's
813 Rue Bienville
New Orleans, LA
866-230-8895
www.arnauds.com

Arnaud's Turtle Soup

1 gallon water
3 pounds turtle meat
3 bay leaves
3 whole cloves
zest of 1 lemon, finely chopped
1 tablespoon kosher salt
1/2 teaspoon whole black peppercorns
1 cup unsalted butter
2/3 cup all purpose flour
2 stalks celery, chopped
2 medium onions, chopped
1 small green bell pepper, stemmed, seeded, de-ribbed and chopped
2 cloves garlic, finely chopped
1/2 teaspoon fresh thyme
1/2 teaspoon chopped fresh marjoram
1 cup dry sherry
2 tablespoons Worcestershire sauces
1 cup tomato puree
1 teaspoon salt-free Creole seasoning
1/2 teaspoon Tabasco Sauce
2 hard cooked eggs, chopped
leaves from 1 bunch of flat-leaf parsley, well washed and chopped
4 cups loosely packed fresh baby spinach, well washed and chopped

In a large stock pot, cover the turtle meat with water and add the bay leaves, cloves, lemon zest, salt and black peppercorns. Place over high heat and bring to a boil. Then immediately reduce the heat so the water simmers gently. Cook slowly for two hours. Strain the stock, reserving the liquid and the meat separately. If necessary, add additional water or meat stock to make three quarts. When cool enough to handle, chop and shred the meat into small pieces and set aside. In a large saucepan, use the butter and flour to make a medium-dark roux the color of a well-used penny. When the roux reaches the correct color, add the celery, onions, bell pepper, garlic, and cook. Stir occasionally until the vegetables are soft. About 7 minutes. Add the thyme, marjoram, sherry, Worcestershire sauce and tomato puree and bring the mixture to a boil. Lower the heat and add the Creole seasoning and Tabasco. Whisk in the reserved stock and add the turtle meat. Simmer the mixture stirring occasionally for about 30 minutes. Taste for seasoning and adjust with salt, pepper and Tabasco Sauce as desired. Add the egg, parsley and spinach leaves and simmer for 10 minutes more. Serve in wide shallow bowls.

Joshua
Happy Father's Day
Daddy
Love, Joshua

TIME CAPSULE CO.
Our Wedding

Lagniappe

Artichoke Balls
Oyster Patties
Strawberry and Spinach Salad
Nwankpa's Pea Cakes
Arroz con Pollo
Spinach Dip
Indian Chicken
Potatoes Au Gratin
Beef Burgundy
Peach Ice Cream

Basil Leaf:
Jasmine Tea Steamed Bass

The Defiant Tree

Mrs. Maria and her husband were allowed back to their New Orleans area home in September after Hurricane Katrina. They surveyed the damage and realized how lucky they were to even have a home. The wind had caused a great deal of roof damage to homes, and there was extensive tree damage in the area. Unfortunately, their bitter orange tree was one of the casualties. It had been knocked down by the wind and was lying on its side. The entire family was disappointed that they lost their bitter orange tree but certainly knew they were fortunate their losses were not greater.

How quickly a simple thing like a tree can evoke emotion! The family reminisced about the times that neighborhood children would creep into Mrs. Maria's back yard and pick the brightly colored oranges from the tree. She would watch as they tried to be sneaky and take a few home. Most kids can't resist the chance to stop and peel them to take a taste. Mrs. Maria would watch and simply smile and anticipate their response. "UGHHHH, these are terrible!"

And yes, alone, those oranges are terrible, tangy, sour and bitter, but they make a fabulous seasoning blend! Every holiday season, Mrs. Maria's family makes its own mojo seasoning for the roasted pig on Christmas Day. Alas, there would be no mojo this year.

Shortly after surveying the rest of the hurricane damaged area, Mrs. Maria and her family were required to leave town again because of Hurricane Rita's approach. They waited anxiously to return home and when they did, they were delighted! The bitter orange tree was standing straight up and it still had a few oranges on its battered branches. "It's a miracle! How could that happen?" No one really knows, but at Christmas this year, the mojo was better than ever!

Kelly's Story

Kelly, like many other New Orleanians, assumed this evacuation would be like the last. She expected a few days of rest out of town, rather than an extended stay out of state. She sent her teenage daughter for a weekend with friends in Houston, packed up a few personal items, left the cats food and water.

Kelly realized very quickly after speaking with her business partner Bank, she needed to return to New Orleans and save her cats! A friend also left his dog behind, so together with another friend they planned a rescue mission.

They put together a team in a canoe and began the journey to her New Orleans home. Early in the trip, Kelly knew the rescue mission would require physical strength, as well as mental strength. The two mile canoe trip took over three hours, and it was all overwhelming for everyone involved.

When the rescue team arrived at Kelly's home, they were happy to find the cats safe. The two cats were obviously traumatized, but had made their way to the top of the kitchen cabinets and were eager to get out of their wet environment. Her friend's dog was also safe. Happily, the rescue boat was filled with people, a dog, and two cats that were just happy to be safe.

When she returned to safety, Kelly was able to find a vet that took great care returning her two cats to health. Next she contacted her daughter, and broke the bad news about their home. Her daughter's strength throughout the conversation was inspiring and relieved Kelly.

After the first difficult conversation, Kelly began a series of conversations that all proved to be challenging. After seeing homes underwater, breathing the heavy air and just knowing the scope of the damage, Kelly was exhausted, but she knew her friends and neighbors should be notified.

Kelly began to post her cell phone number on the internet. The calls were immediate; neighbors she never knew were asking about their homes. Often people would deny her comments were true; others would yell, but more would cry. Forever, Kelly will be known as the person who told them everything was gone!

Artichoke Balls

1 (14 ounce) can hearts of artichokes
1 cup seasoned bread crumbs
2 raw eggs
2 tablespoons olive oil
2 tablespoons lemon juice
3 or 4 cloves of garlic, put through press
2 tablespoons freshly grated Parmesan cheese

Drain and mash artichoke hearts thoroughly. Add remaining ingredients except Parmesan cheese. Mix thoroughly. Refrigerate at least four hours or overnight. Form into small balls, then roll in Parmesan cheese. May be served cold or heated until light brown in a hot oven (400 degrees). Since the balls freeze well, they may be made in advance and used as needed.

Oyster Patties

24 Pepperidge Farm pastry shells
24 Louisiana oysters with oyster liquid
4 stalks celery, minced
2 cloves garlic, minced
1 bunch scallions, minced
1/3 bunch parsley, minced
2 tablespoons butter

Bake pastry shells according to directions on the box. Let cool, then remove pastry from inside the shells with a fork. Put aside in a bowl for later use. Melt butter in skillet. Saute celery until slightly soft, then add scallions. Saute for about 3 minutes, then add garlic, stirring constantly. After mixture becomes sold add the insides of the patty shells and water from the oysters. Consistency should be like a thick gravy. If necessary, add water to keep the mixture from becoming too thick. When the pastry mixture cooks down, add the oysters and cook until the butter rises to the top, about 10 to 15 minutes. Oysters will shrink when cooked. Add the parsley, and stir for about 1 minute. Fill each patty shell with at least one oyster and some of the mixture. Put pastry top on to cover. The patty shells can be filled and refrigerated, then warmed in the oven at 300 degrees when ready to serve.

Strawberry and Spinach Salad

1 bag fresh baby spinach
1/4 cup roasted walnuts
1 pint Louisiana strawberries sliced
1/4 cup Balsamic vinegar
4 tablespoons strawberry wine
1 1/2 cups olive oil
1 tablespoon thyme, chopped
salt and pepper to taste
goat cheese

Whisk together vinegar, oil, wine, thyme salt and pepper. Toss with spinach walnuts, and strawberries. Garnish with goat cheese.

Nwankpa's Pea Cakes

8 ounces dried black eye peas
1 cup water, divided
1/2 onion, diced
1/4 teaspoon salt
1 can tomato paste
corn or peanut oil

Soak peas in water for ten minutes. Stir and rub the peas by hand to remove all of the outer coatings. Place beans in a blender with 1/4 cup water, onions, salt and tomato paste. The consistency should be thick. Add more water if it seems too thick. In a heavy pot heat 3 inches of corn or peanut oil until hot. Drop spoonfuls of the bean mixture into the hot oil and fry. Turn the cakes regularly to ensure browning throughout. Do not burn! Drain on a paper towel and serve with rice and plantains.

Arroz con Pollo

Mojo is a tart Cuban condiment made with bitter orange that is often used on grilled meats and seafood.

12 pieces of chicken
2 large onions
3 packages Pearl rice
6 pieces garlic
2 small cans tomato sauce
2 cups minced ham
3 cups Vino Seco
1 tablespoons pepper
3 teaspoons paprika
1 1/3 cups of olive oil
2 large bell peppers
12 minced olives
1/4 cup ketchup
10-12 cups chicken broth
saffron to taste
Bijol to taste
3 Tablespoons salt
canned asparagus
LeSeur Petit Pois
whole pimentos

Season chicken the night before with mojo and garlic powder. Begin by browning the chicken in olive oil. When done, remove from pan. Brown ham in same pan and cook down. Obtain sofrito by scraping the bottom of the pan. Add rice and remaining ingredients. Cook in 325 degree preheated oven until rice is fully cooked, about 45 minutes. Garnish with canned asparagus, petit pois and pimentos.

Spinach Dip

2 boxes chopped spinach
1 (8 ounce) sour cream
1 (8 ounce) cream cheese
1/4 cup Parmesan cheese
1/2 chopped yellow onion (Vidalia)
1/2 stick butter
1 (8 ounce) Monterey Jack cheese
1 can artichoke hearts (drained)
crushed red pepper, salt to taste

Saute butter and onions. Add ingredients one at a time: Spinach, cream cheese, sour cream, Parmesan cheese, artichoke hearts, 4 ounces Monterey Jack cheese, seasonings. Top with remaining cheese and microwave or bake in 350 degree oven until top turns light brown.

Indian Chicken

6 chicken legs, skin removed
6 chicken thighs, skin removed
5 whole cardamom
1 1/2 teaspoons tumeric powder
1 teaspoon cumin powder
3/4 teaspoons coriander powder
1/2 teaspoon paprika
1 teaspoon red chili powder
1 pinch asafoetida
1 large onion, chopped
1 square ginger root, peeled and chopped
10 garlic cloves peeled
1 cup water, more if necessary
2 large green peppers, cut into large chunks
4-5 bay leaves
8 whole cloves
3-4 cinnamon sticks
1/4 cup lemon juice, more if desired
1 teaspoon butter
chopped coriander

In a pot toast the cardamom, tumeric, cumin, coriander, paprika, chili powder and asafoetida until fragrant. Add oil and fry chicken. Add onions, garlic and ginger. This should create a paste around the chicken. Add water, bay leaves, cloves, cinnamon sticks, lemon juice, and salt. Cook covered on low heat for 30 minutes. Before serving, stir in butter and garnish with chopped fresh coriander. Serve over rice

Potatoes Au Gratin

2 tablespoons butter
2 tablespoons flour
1/2 teaspoon salt
1 1/2 cup milk
1/4 pounds cheese
1 1/2 pounds sliced potatoes
1/4 cup bread crumbs

Melt butter, blend flour and salt. Stir until smooth. Turn heat low and slowly add milk stirring constantly. Cook and stir until thick and smooth. Remove from heat. Add cheese and stir until melted. Arrange potatoes in 1 1/2 quart casserole. Pour cheese sauce over potatoes top with crumbs. Dot with additional butter. Bake in 350 degrees for 15 or 20 minutes.

Beef Burgundy

4 tablespoons bacon grease
7 medium onions sliced
2 pounds lean beef cubed (boneless chuck)
3 tablespoons flour
1 teaspoon salt
1/2 teaspoon pepper
1/2 teaspoon majoram
1/2 teaspoon thyme
1 (6 ounce) can sliced mushrooms
1 (10 ounce) can undiluted beef bouillon
2 cups dry burgundy
1 teaspoon liquid gravy seasoning

Saute onions for eight minutes in 2 tablespoons of grease. Remove onions from heat. Add remaining grease to the pot and brown meat cubes. Return onions to the pan and toss in the flour. Add salt, pepper, marjoram, and thyme. Add 1 cup of wine. Bring to a boil reduce heat and simmer for three hours until the meat falls apart and is tender. Add the remaining wine, mushrooms and gravy seasoning. Bring to a boil. Reduce heat and simmer for 45 minutes.

Peach Ice Cream

2 tablespoons unflavored gelatin
3 cups milk
2 cups sugar
1/4 teaspoon salt
6 eggs
1 1/2 quarts light cream
1 (3 3/4 ounce) instant vanilla pudding mix
5 teaspoon vanilla
1 quart pureed fresh peaches

Soften gelatin in 1/2 cup cold milk. Scald the mixture and stir 1 1/2 cup milk into gelatin mixture until it dissolves. Add sugar and salt, stirring until dissolved. Add remaining milk. Beat eggs at high speed for five minutes. Add light cream, pudding mix, vanilla and gelatin mixture. Stir in peaches. Freeze in ice cream maker.

Jasmine Tea Steamed Bass

Basil Leaf
1438 S Carrollton Ave,
New Orleans, LA 70118
504-862-9001

1.5 pound whole fish cleaned (bass or red snapper)
1-2 pickled plums, salted
1 1/2 tablespoons mushroom soy sauce, or light soy sauce
black pepper to taste
2 tablespoons butter, sliced
1/2 stalk celery, sliced on bias
1 piece fresh ginger, finely diced
3 cups water
2 tablespoons jasmine tea leaves

Sauce

3 tablespoons soy sauce
2 drops sesame oil
1/2 teaspoon fresh ginger, diced
1 grilled whole jalapeno pepper, thinly sliced

Bring water and jasmine tea leaves to a boil while cleaning and preparing fish. Place fish in steaming tray. Rub both sides of the fish with mashed pickled plum and sprinkle with black pepper as well. Place butter, ginger and celery slices over the top of the fish. Lightly pour soy sauce over the fish. Steam over tea for 15 minutes and serve immediately with dipping sauce.

To make the dipping sauce combine soy sauce, sesame oil, ginger and jalapeno. If you don't care for spicy food, leave out the jalapeno.

Staying Behind

September 22nd was the eighth anniversary of Basil Leaf. Unfortunately, with the stresses of hurricane Katrina, the usual anniversary celebration was missed. In fact, a week after the special occasion, the owners and staff realized they missed the date!

Luckily, the restaurant sustained very little storm damage and avoided some of the looting problems others in the area experienced. Bank, one of the owners of Basil Leaf, stayed behind to keep an eye on the neighborhood.

There are several restaurants on the block, and Bank was the only owner around. Armed with signs displaying, "Now serving bullets." Bank stood his ground and began neighborhood watch. He scared off looters with signs in the windows and his commanding presence at a candlelit table outside of Basil Leaf. He was in control of most of the immediate area.

On Tuesday after the storm, he knew that food would begin to defrost and spoil if he didn't cook it soon. So Bank fired up the butane tanks and cooked for the neighborhood, 400 pounds of crabmeat, 150 dozen soft shell crabs and gave away as much food as he possible could.

There was a point in time that Bank knew he had to get out of New Orleans. He packed up a bag containing a few personal items: an old watch, antique coins and his mother's recipe book. To the untrained eye, the recipe book appears to only contain grocery lists and commentary but to Bank, it is everything. His mother simply included a list of ingredients and a description of what the final dish should taste like. The steps in between he learned at his mother's side; he would never consider leaving that book behind.

As Bank fled the flooded city, he witnessed a few last neighborhood residents holding out. He offered them keys to the restaurant and said, "Good Luck, and if you need anything, help yourself." He wanted to make sure that the residents had food and water. He also placed bags of dry goods and can goods on the curb, so that people in need could help themselves.

Bank's cooking and concern for nearby residents has led to a greater unity in the neighborhood. The restaurateurs on the block are now all very close, and the neighborhood watch system continues. In fact, when one restaurant runs out of flour, the other comes to the rescue, and at some points, they are even sharing staff to keep up with the demand.

Eight Months Later

Dear Reader,

You may ask yourself, "What is it like there now?"

Eight months, ten months and twelve months later, progress is extremely slow. Homes are still filled with moldy furniture, families are still displaced, and trash is still piled up in neighborhood streets.

Thousands of homes and business still need repairs and contractors are difficult to find. Construction prices have skyrocketed and there are bidding wars for the few available apartments. Traffic is still out of control, every conversation still begins with, "Before Katrina," and the smell of mold is still clinging to the air.

Unfortunately, there appears to be no end in sight and hurricane season is upon us again.

Our homes and lives are in shambles and our futures are uncertain. Local, state, and national leaders cannot agree on a plan and homeowners are forced to endure the consequences of the politicians' inaction.

Just because a home was flooded, and is uninhabitable, and government leaders cannot decide if a neighborhood will be rebuilt, it doesn't mean the mortgage company isn't asking for a check each month.

We've tried to lighten our mood with food and festivals. Mardi Gras was the best I can ever remember, French Quarter fest was a much needed break from reality, and Jazz Fest was something we all had to experience once more. We seek comfort in our food and our heritage, but that alone is not enough to rebuild a city.

Lately, it seems as if our situation is no longer national headline news. Some out-of-towners believe we are getting too much coverage; they're tired of hearing it. That must mean everything is resolved right? That is definitely not the case! We're not OK, but we are getting better.

Please don't forget about us. Don't forget about the families who lost loved ones, the people who lost their homes and the reasons why this disaster happened. Keep in mind the ruined family photos, recipes and other priceless life possessions that are now only memories as a result of this unfortunate event. Don't forget about the businesses that can't survive or the schools that are now closed.

The number of people outside of the region who believe that New Orleans and the surrounding areas are back to normal amazes me. This by no means is true; this is not normal, and life is not normal anymore. Before Katrina, it was not normal to share a one bedroom apartment with 14 relatives, it was not normal to see devastation everywhere you turn and it was not normal to wonder if your friends have relocated or just haven't been found.

Many New Orleanians feel forgotten by the rest of the nation because they see no real progress and feel nobody cares. The millions and billions of dollars sent to the area to assist in the rebuilding process are being spent but little, if any, has made it into the hands of homeowners. Many local residents wonder, "What if this were New York? What if this were San Francisco? Would they be in the same situation eight, ten or twelve months later?"

Many outsiders don't want to hear the truth, it's depressing. Yes it is! We live it every day. It can wear you down. But that doesn't mean if we ignore the situation, it will go away. We can't pretend that our lives have returned to Technicolor, but we can make it happen if we rebuild with a genuine commitment.

The citizens who are back in New Orleans are making a daily sacrifice for a home they love and a culture worth saving. We sacrifice our sanity by listening to the bickering, finger pointing and politics while we look devastation in the face, and see little progress. Our struggle is not over.

We mourn the loss of our fellow citizens and worry about the loss of our unique culture. We work hard every day to pick up the pieces of our lives and rebuild the city we love, with or without help.

We enjoy what is left of our city by dancing in the streets at festivals, dining with family and friends and reveling with strangers at Mardi Gras. That is what keeps us going and that is what makes us who we are.

Yes, we have been hit hard, and yes it will be a long road ahead. Despite all that has been thrown our way, we still maintain hope. Hope that New Orleans will once again be a great place to live. Hope that our fellow citizens can rebuild their lives in the neighborhoods they once knew. Hope that a disaster such as this doesn't happen to anyone else, ever. And hope that during next Mardi Gras and Jazz Fest we can celebrate with friends, family, neighbors, tourists and strangers.

What will we be celebrating? Us! You, me, life, food everything and anything! Maybe we will even be celebrating the New Normal, and maybe we will actually like it. With help, support and understanding, we can do it. New Orleans is our home, and as we all know, "There's no place like home!"

We are traveling the long road back. Care to join us?

Coalition to Restore Coastal Louisiana

IMPLICATIONS OF COASTAL LAND LOSS

In recent years, dire predictions of catastrophic consequences have fueled Louisiana's efforts to restore our failing coast. Comprising nearly 1/3 of our state's land area and home to 2/3 of Louisiana's residents, Louisiana's coastal zone has been battered by hurricanes and shaped to meet the demands of modern development.

Louisiana's coastal wetlands stand on the verge of collapse. In the past 50 years, more than 1500 square miles of coastal Louisiana have been lost. Without immediate and decisive action, Louisiana stands to lose an additional 1000 square miles of land, an area the size of Rhode Island, by the year 2050. This land is not only an important habitat for fish and wildlife, it provides and indispensable storm buffer for communities, transportation routes and energy infrastructure.

Wetlands and barrier islands protect billions of dollars worth of oil and gas infrastructure from wave and storm damage. This disappearing land is a key part of the nation's energy system. Nearly 25% of all the oil and gas consumed in America and 80% of the nation's offshore oil and gas travels through Louisiana's wetlands. As wetlands and barrier islands erode, our oil and gas infrastructure will become exposed to open water and increasingly susceptible storm damage. At a time when our nation is attempting to move toward a self-sufficient energy policy, the rich resources of Louisiana will become increasingly more important to the future of the United States.

Louisiana's barrier islands and wetland shorelines protect navigation channels, anchorages and ports from winds, waves, storms and hurricanes. Louisiana's ports provide the nation with approximately 20% of the nation's foreign waterborne commerce. They contribute billions to local economies and provide Louisiana with thousands of jobs. Without the protection of our rapidly eroding coastal wetlands and barrier islands, 155 miles of waterways will be exposed to open water in 50 years and billions of taxpayer dollars will have to be spent on increased dredging and maintenance costs.

Louisiana's wetlands provide critical habitat and food resources for some of our nation's most productive recreational and commercial fisheries. The abundance of our fisheries is generated by the millions of acres of coastal marsh that is used as a nursery by young fish and shellfish. Wetlands also serve as natural filters of sewage and other pollutants introduced through drainage basins and the larger watershed region. As our wetlands and estuarine marshes collapse, saltwater intrusion will escalate salinity levels and disturb the delicate balance between fresh and salt water that support the bountiful fisheries of Louisiana.

Wetlands and barrier islands form a natural buffer zone that absorbs storm surges and blunts the force of high winds. Scientists estimate that every 2.7 miles of wetlands absorb one foot of storm surge.

As the barrier islands and wetlands erode, south Louisiana communities will be exposed to the direct brunt of storms and hurricanes. If wetlands and barrier islands continue to erode as projected, more than 2 million people living in south Louisiana could be subjected to more frequent and severe flooding.

The frequency of flooding along Louisiana's coastal zone has already caused some insurance companies to discontinue coverage and cease issuing policies. If we do not change our present course and rebuild this buffer zone, severe flooding will endanger all long-term investments in south Louisiana.

The implications are indeed catastrophic, but they are not inevitable. The decisions we make today will determine if future generations will enjoy the same coastal bounty that has made this region a national treasure. Considering what is at stake we do not have the luxury of time or inaction. Together, we must make a dedicated and united commitment to the security, prosperity and future of south Louisiana.

MISSION AND GOALS

The Coalition to Restore Coastal Louisiana is a non-profit advocacy organization whose mission is the preservation, restoration and responsible stewardship of the coastal wetlands, waters and barrier shorelines of coastal Louisiana.

The goal of the Coalition is to reverse the pattern of net land loss in coastal Louisiana and to reestablish a sustainable balance to its geologic processes and communities. In pursuit of this goal, the Coalition advocates for the implementation of sound coastal policies and monitors coastal activities to ensure that stringent regulations and enforcement policies are maintained.

Fulfilling our role as responsible stewards of Louisiana's rich coastal wetlands, we facilitate and fund actual restoration activity and work diligently to raise awareness and educate others about the importance of preserving and restoring coastal Louisiana.

The Coalition works to match key financial resources with unique opportunities and diverse partnerships to leverage our efforts in the fight against coastal land loss. We play a unique and effective role in forming these partnerships and direct their efforts to ensure that they produce meaningful results.

Through these actions, the Coalition works to shape the way people approach development of our coastal area and the way we manage the Mississippi River corridor. This multifaceted and comprehensive approach to coastal restoration demonstrates our steadfast commitment and distinguishes the Coalition to Restore Coastal Louisiana from any other civic or environmental group.

Maque Choux

Louisiana Bistro
337 Dauphine Street
New Orleans, LA 70112
504-525-3335

6 ears corn
2 onions, diced
6 jalapenos, diced
3 tablespoons garlic, minced
2 cups stock or water
2 ounces cream
1/2 cup scallion rounds

The key to this dish is the cutting of the veggies. Shuck the corn and remove all strings. Holding the ear on end slice through half of the kernel all the way down the ear, effectively cutting off the top half of each kernel. Proceed all the way around the ear. Then cut off the bottom half of the kernels. Each kernel is then cut in half which will later allow starch to easily leak from the kernels. Remove the stem and quarter each jalapeno lengthways. Remove the white embanes and all of the seeds, thereby removing most, but not all, of the heat. Dice the "meat" of the jalapeno the same size as the corn kernels. Dice the onions the same size.

Heat a large skillet to high and begin to saute all vegetables except the scallions. The key is to constantly stir the corn under high heat until a light starch layer of brown begins to form on the bottom of the pan. This brown has important flavor. Add small amounts of the water and stock to loosen the fond (brown stuff) from the bottom and proceed sautéing until more brown forms. Repeat with the liquid. This process is similar to the method for making risotto, using stages of liquid and constant motion to cause starch to thicken the self producing sauce. When corn is cooked through but not mushy (this should not be anything like creamed corn) add scallions and a touch of cream. Season with salt and cayenne. This will hold hot for quite awhile. Goes great as a seafood side dish.

Lagniappe- such as this recipe, is a little something extra for you to enjoy!

Louisiana Resources

Mr. Lake's Forum
http://www.network54.com/Index/10892

Gumbo Pages
www.gumbopages.com

The Weather Channel
www.theweatherchannel.com

Fonville Photography
www.spiart.com

Tate Tullier Photography
www.tatetullier.com

Food Products

Crystal Hot Sauce
www.baumerfoods.com

Savoie's Products
www.realcajun.com

Wistaria Sweet Potatoes
wistaria@bayou.com

New Orleans Overnight
www.nuawlins.com

Mrs. Wheat's Meat Pies
www.mrswheatsfood.com

Boscoli Foods
www.boscoli.com

Steen's Cane Syrup
www.steensyrup.com

Zapp's Chips
www.zapps.com

Leidenheimer French Bread
www.leidenheimer.com

Nectar Soda
www.nectarsoda.com

Pat Obrien's Hurricane
www.patobriens.com

Café Du Monde
www.cafedumonde.com

Blue Plate Mayonaise
www.luzianne.com

Community Coffee
www.communitycoffee.com

Tabasco sauce
www.tabasco.com

Tony Cachere's Seasoning
www.tonychachere.com

H.J. Bergeron Pecan's
hjblesjr@tlxnet.net

Blue Runner's Red Beans
www.bluerunnerfoods.com

Zatarain's
www.zatarain.com

Creole Cream Cheese
www.jfolse.com

Abita Brewing Company
www.abita.com

Cajun Power Sauces
www.cajunpowersauce.com

Gagliano Farms
www.creoletomatoes.com

Rex Fine Foods
www.rexfoods.com

Meat Products

Bellue's Cajun Foods
www.belluescajuncuisine.com

Benoit's Country Meats
www.benoitscajunmeats.com

Chris' Specialty Meats
www.chrisspecialtymeats.com

Vaucresson Sausage
www.vaucressonsausage.com

Abita Quail
www.abitaquailfarm.com

Seafood

Louisiana Seafood Seafood
www.louisianaseafood.com

Catfish Wholesale
www.catfishwholesale.com

P & J Oyster Company
www.oysterlover.com

Fruge Cajun Crawfish
www.cajuncrawfish.com

Bayouland Seafood
www.bayoulandseafood.com

Sweets

Manny Randazzo's King Cakes
www.mannyrandazzo.com

Gambino's Bakery
www.gambinos.com

Aunt Sally's Pralines
www.auntsallys.com

Domino Sugar
www.dominosugar.com

Elmer Candy
www.elmercandy.com

Roman Candy
www.romancandy.com

Other

Toulouse Royale
www.neworleanstogo.com

Contributions, Photographs and Inspiration

Moto Restaurant
Catherine Bergeron
Ashley Coates
Aimee Harris
Stephen and Dawn Oster
Karen Skal
Megan Karlton
Bayonna Restaurant
Mandina's Restaurant
Janet and Rick Sins
Randee Joffrion
Whole Foods Market
Denice and Billy Ducote
George and Kathleen Mayer
Fannie Moore
Claire Simno
Beth Blistan
Daniel Adam Leyten
Mr. Lake's Forum Members
George Sins
Lilette Restaurant
Bob Rue
Frank Nett
Frank Speyer
Meg Casler
Chuck Taggert
Pam Becker
Romney Stubbs
Karen Bias
Julie Schiffer
Renee and Edmond Haase
Marianne Garon
Karen Junot
Sheron Hebert
Peristyle Restaurant
Henry Harmison
Pete Vasquez
Wendy Gaudin
Paulette Beatty
Tom Eisler
Ardie Greenamyer
MiMi Mary Cammarata
Sam Cammarata
Pauline Troxclair
Annie Gimoen-Ducote
Charlie Company- 769th Engineer Battalion
Nicole Labadot
Laura Chitty
Laura Lyons
Marian Needham
Verlyn Latino
Dan Bode
Dale Moore
Margie Landry
Chaplain Bob
Catherine Campanella
George and Kathleen Mayer
Gerald Freyder
Lisa Dwyer
Tammy Arrigo
Eric Milliken
Keith Bird
Tate Tullier
Aaron Cyrex
Restaurant August
Lynn Long
Café Giovanni
Joan Phillips
The Windsor Court
Herbsaint
Maria's Multiregional Cuisine
Dorignacs Food Store
Angelo Broccato
Mr. Jezz
Gabrielle Restaurant
Drago's Restaurant
Jams Poboys
Wolfe's of New Orleans
Peristyle Restaurant
Gregory St. Pierre
Hotel St. Marie
Arnauds Restaurant
Maria Castillio
Marisa and Steve Suarez
Bennett Nwankpa
Minati Biswas
Miriam Garrett
Basil Leaf
Kelly Hotard
Siam Bank
Scott Bell
Danny and Cristy Suarez
Maria and Sergio Castillo
Steve Kleinpeter
Kevin Himel
Amy Waller
Big Al
Katherine Sins
Loren Leblanc
Rob Dahmes
Louisiana Bistro

And all of you who supplied photography, inspiration and support that are far too many to list in such a short book!

Index

A

APPETIZERS
Artichoke Balls 201
Audrey's Stuffed Artichokes 65
Cajun Fire and Ice Pickles 45
Chile Con Queso 87
Dawn's Fresh Salsa 87
Drago's Grilled Oysters 153
Guacamole 88
Janet's Marinated Cheese 97
Old English Petit Fours 33
Oyster Patties 201
Pepper Jelly 179
Roasted Garlic Spread 77
Spinach Dip 203
Tostitos with Salsa Jelly and Margarita 5
ARTICHOKES
Artichoke Balls 201
Audrey's Stuffed Artichokes 65
Green Bean and Artichoke Casserole 193
Spinach Dip 203

B

BEANS AND PEAS
Black Eyed Peas 23
Captain's Red Beans & Rice 150
Green Bean and Artichoke Casserole 193
Marinated Green Beans 98
Nwankpa's Pea Cakes 202
Rocky and Carlo's Inspired Green Beans 161
Taco Pie 89
BEEF
Beef Burgundy 205
Beef Tenderloin 35
Danno's Corned Beef 67
Grillades 169
Jams Roast Beef 163
Marisol Menudo 91
Taco Pie 89
BEVERAGES
Brandy Milk Punch 26
Café Brulot 110
Dawn's Chocolate Martini 37
Frozen Strawberry Margarita 90
George's Famous Bloody Mary 48
Irish Coffee 68
Kaluha 183
Kirk's Hot Chocolate Mix 181
Mimosas 170
Nectar Soda 100
Ramos Gin Fizz 37
Red Hot Punch 194
Satsuma Sipper 162
Sazerac Cocktail 151
Tammy's Champagne Punch 110
BREADS
Auntie Nika's Cafeteria Style Rolls 191
Cornbread 25
Cornbread Casserole 151
Danno's Muffuletta Bread 47
Mini Cinis 170
Sweet Potato Muffins 129
Tea Scones 111
BREAKFAST AND BRUNCH
Baked Grits 170
Chocolate Muffin 185
Grillades 169
Haitian Fain Patate 131
Mini Cinis 170
Smoked Mushroom and Parma Prosciutto Frittata 173
Sweet Bacon for a Crowd 169
Wolfe's Crawfish and Andouille Sausage 174

C

CAKES
Carrot 118
Chocolate, Chocolate and Chocolate 121
Easy Birthday Doberge 119
Pontchatoula Strawberry Shortcake 119
CANDY
Chocolate Truffles 110
Granny's Peanut Brittle 179
Heavenly Hash 180
Peanut Butter Balls 180
Peanut Butter Fudge 181
Turtles 183
CASSEROLES
Aunt Verlyn's Cabbage Casserole 68
Cornbread Casserole 151
Granny Gahn's Shrimp-Stuffed Mirliton 193
Green Bean and Artichoke Casserole 193
Oyster Dressing Alzina 192
Patsy's Cornbread Dressing 192
Seafood Casserole 58
Squash Casserole 160
CHICKEN
Arroz con Pollo 203
Blackened Chicken Salad Sandwiches 107
Chicken Fricassee 159
Daddy's Jambalaya xiii
Indian Chicken 204
Mexican Style Chicken 88
Mrs. Fannie's Fried Chicken 45
Okra Gumbo 189
Oyster Dressing Alzina 192
The Academy's Greek Pasta Salad 99
CHOCOLATE
Chocolate, Chocolate and Chocolate Cake 121
Chocolate Malt Creme Brule 123
Chocolate Muffin 185
Chocolate Sweet Dough Pie 79
Chocolate Truffles 110
Congo Squares 184
Dawn's Chocolate Martini 37
Easy Birthday Doberge Cake 119
Heavenly Hash 180
Kirk's Hot Chocolate Mix 181
Mississippi Mud Pie 120
Turtles 183
White Chocolate Chip Cookies 117
COOKIES
Congo Squares 184
Dainty Oatmeal Lace 109
Gooch Cookies 184
Grandma Cookies 183
White Chocolate Chip 117
CORN
Cornbread Casserole 151
Crawfish Boil 75
Creole Maque Choux 25
Maque Choux 213
Shrimp Chowder a la Marianne 56
Vodoo Shrimp 102
CORNBREAD
Cornbread Casserole 151
Patsy's Cornbread Dressing 192
CRAB
Crabmeat Au Gratin 58
Flash Fried Louisiana Softshell Crabs 101

Seafood Casserole 58
Seafood Fettuccini 56

CRAWFISH
Corn and Crawfish Soup 76
Crawfish Boil 75
Down Home Crawfish Pie 82
Reneetouffe 55
Seafood Casserole 58
Seafood Fettuccini 56
Wolfe's Crawfish and Andouille Sausage 174

D

DESSERTS
Blueberry Pie 118
Carrot Cake 118
Chaplain Bob's World Famous Apple Cake 100
Chocolate, Chocolate and Chocolate Cake 121
Chocolate Malt Creme Brule 123
Chocolate Muffin 185
Chocolate Truffles 110
Congo Squares 184
Dainty Oatmeal Lace Cookies 109
deBess Bread Pudding 161
E-Ema's Pecan Pie Tarts 108
Easy Birthday Doberge Cake 119
Gooch Cookies 184
Grandma Cookies 183
Granny's Peanut Brittle 179
Haitian Pain Patate 131
Heavenly Hash 180
Italian Fig Cookies 70
Italian Sesame Seed Cookies 69
King Cake 46
Lemon Icebox Pie 122
Mini Cinis 170
Mini Strawberry Pies 108
Mississippi Mud Pie 120
Nanny's Banana Pudding 26
Peach Ice Cream 205
Peanut Butter Balls 180
Peanut Butter Fudge 181
Pontchatoula Strawberry Shortcake 119
Praline Cheesecake 152
Red Velvet Bites 36
Sopapillas 89
Strawberry and Fig Jam 109
Sweet Dough Pies 78
Tea Scones 111
Tiramisu 194
Turtles 183
White Chocolate Chip Cookies 117

DRESSING
Granny Gahn's Shrimp-Stuffed Mirliton 193
Green Bean and Artichoke Casserole 193
Oyster Dressing Alzina 192
Patsy's Cornbread Dressing 192

DUCK
Duck Confit with Savory Spinach and Mushroom Vinaigrette 49
Grilled Roasted Duck Breast 142

F

FISH
Jasmine Tea Steamed Bass 207
Pecan Redfish 140
Sautéed Catfish 124
Seared Tuna 39

J

JAMS AND JELLIES
Pepper Jelly 179
Strawberry and Fig Jam 109

O

OKRA
Creole Maque Choux 25
Okra Gumbo 189

OYSTERS
Drago's Grilled Oysters 153
Hot Oyster Dip 57
Oyster Dressing Alzina 192
Oyster Patties 201

P

PASTA
Junk and Cheese 160
Seafood Fettuccini 56
The Academy's Greek Pasta Salad 99

PEANUT BUTTER
Granny's Peanut Brittle 179
Peanut Butter Balls 180
Peanut Butter Fudge 181

PIES
Blueberry Pie 118
E-Ema's Pecan Pie Tarts 108
Lemon Icebox Pie 122
Mini Strawberry Pies 108
Mississippi Mud Pie 120
Sweet Potato Pie 131

PORK
Green Pork Tenderloin 100
Panned Pork Chops 24
Sweet Bacon for a Crowd 169

R

RESTAURANT RECIPES
Arnaud's Turtle Soup 195
Asparagus Soup 59
Chocolate Malt Creme Brule 123
Chocolate Muffin 185

Down Home Crawfish Pie 82
Drago's Grilled Oysters 153
Duck Confit with Savory Spinach and Mushroom Vinaigrette 49
Flash Fried Louisiana Softshell Crabs with Southern Comfort and Tasso Cream Sauce 101
Grilled Shrimp with Coriander Sauce and Black Bean Cake 27
Italian Fig Cookies 70
Italian Sesame Seed Cookies 69
Jams Roast Beef and Gravy by Joe 163
Jasmine Tea Steamed Bass 207
Marisol Menudo 91
Maque Choux 213
Oyster and Artichoke Soup 31
Panned Rabbit with Satusuma Sauce 143
Potato and Leek Soup 133
Salad August 81
Sautéed Catfish with Louisiana Shrimp and Jalapeno Slaw 124
Seared Tuna with Sautéed Greens 39
Smoked Mushroom and Parma Prosciutto Frittata 173
Tea Scones 111
Vodoo Shrimp 102
Wolfe's Crawfish and Andouille Sausage 174

RICE
- Arroz con Pollo 203
- Captain's Red Beans & Rice 150
- Daddy's Jambalaya xiii
- Mother's Club Jambalaya 45

S

SALAD
- Blackened Chicken Salad 107
- Potato Salad 76
- Salad August 81
- Salad of Pomegranates, Green Beans, Jicama and Walnuts 40
- Shrimp Remoulade Salad 34
- Strawberry and Spinach Salad 202
- The Academy's Greek Pasta Salad 99

SALADS
- Creole Tomato Salad 150
- Sensation Salad 159

SANDWICHES
- Blackened Chicken Salad 107
- Green Pork Tenderloin 100
- Muffulettas 48
- Pecan Raisin Pineapple 109
- Pimento Cheese 107

SAUCE
- Praline Sauce 130
- Satusuma Sauce 143
- Southern Comfort and Tasso Cream Sauce 101

SAUCES
- Anchovy Gravy 65
- Mimi Mary's Meat Sauce 66

SAUSAGE
- Black Eyed Peas 23
- Crawfish Boil 75
- Creole Maque Choux 25
- Mimi Mary's Meat Sauce 66
- Mother's Club Jambalaya 45
- Okra Gumbo 189
- Pecan Redfish 140
- Rocky and Carlo's Inspired Green Beans 161
- Smothered Cabbage 24
- Wolfe's Crawfish and Andouille Sausage 174

SHRIMP
- BBQ Shrimp 57
- Granny Gahn's Shrimp-Stuffed Mirliton 193
- Julie's Shrimp Creole 55
- Louisiana Shrimp and Jalapeno Slaw 124
- Seafood Casserole 58
- Shrimp Chowder a la Marianne 56
- Vodoo Shrimp 102

SOUP
- Arnaud's Turtle Soup 195
- Asparagus Soup 59
- Corn and Crawfish Soup 76
- Okra Gumbo 189
- Onion Soup 149
- Potato and Leek Soup 133

STRAWBERRY
- Frozen Strawberry Margarita 90
- Mini Strawberry Pies 108
- Pontchatoula Strawberry Shortcake 119
- Strawberry and Fig Jam 109
- Strawberry and Spinach Salad 202

SWEET DOUGH PIES
- Blackberry 79
- Bouille 78
- Chocolate 79
- Dough Pie Slurry 80
- Fig 78
- Icing 80
- Peach 79
- Pineapple 80

SWEET POTATO
- Gnocchi with Praline Sauce 130
- Haitian Pain Patate 131
- Ravioli 132
- Sweet Potato Crunch 129
- Sweet Potato Muffins 129
- Sweet Potato Pie 131

T

TURKEY
- Cajun Fried Turkey 191

V

VEGETABLES
- Audrey's Stuffed Artichokes 65
- Aunt Verlyn's Cabbage Casserole 68
- Black Eyed Peas 23
- Cajun Fire and Ice Pickles 45
- Cajun Grilled Ratatouille 36
- Coleslaw 98
- Creole Maque Choux 25
- Granny Gahn's Shrimp-Stuffed Mirliton 193
- Green Bean and Artichoke Casserole 193
- Marinated Green Beans 98
- Potatoes Au Gratin 204
- Potato Rockefeller 34
- Potato Salad 76
- Rocky and Carlo's Inspired Green Beans 161
- Smothered Cabbage 24
- Spinach Dip 203
- Squash Casserole 160
- Sweet Potato Crunch 129
- Turnip Greens 151

W

WILD GAME
- Arnaud's Turtle Soup 195
- Deer Sauce Piquante 139
- Fried Alligator 142
- Grilled Roasted Duck Breast 142
- Panned Rabbit Panned Rabbit with Satusuma Sauce 143
- Stewed Squirrel 141
- Sweet Jalapeno Grilled Quail 141

Amy Cyrex Sins is a Loyola University of New Orleans graduate with a degree in Communications. She is a cooking enthusiast who spends every free moment in the kitchen creating wonderful meals for friends and family.

Her specialty is entertaining and creating fun, festive and memorable parties for every occasion. In Amy's kitchen, she incorporates a unique blend of classic local cuisine with emerging culinary trends to create food everyone can appreciate.

She enjoys the distinctive blend of culture, history and cuisine in the daily lives of her fellow New Orleanians. With the fleeting days, she becomes even more nostalgic for the flavors of her childhood and the stories of times past.

Amy was inspired to write her first cookbook after the events of Hurricane Katrina ravaged her home and her city. The one thing she lost that was missed most of all was her collection of handwritten recipes passed on from family and friends.

The spirit, resiliency, and will of she and her fellow citizens will be evident in the pages of Ruby Slippers.